Chinatown County

Author Bruce Russell as stand-in for Chinatown's Jake Gittes,
"He-of-the-Nicked-Nose"

Chinatown County

The Sell-Out of Marina del Rey

BRUCE RUSSELL

*To Carla, whose dedication
to preserving the recreational
Marina is a source
of inspiration.*

CHINATOWN COUNTY:
The Sell-Out of Marina del Rey
By Bruce Russell

Copyright © 2014 by Bruce Russell. All rights reserved.

ISBN: 978-1-304-85094-2

First Printing. Printed in the United States of America.
Cover photograph, and book design by Kate Doll.
Photograph of author: Ivor Davis

TABLE OF CONTENTS

CHAPTER ONE

The Sell-Out of Marina del Rey

Early in the nineteen-hundreds Los Angeles officialdom engaged in such a seamy act of subterfuge that it became part of the city legend. The city was moving rapidly towards the sprawling megalopolis it is today and the insignificant Los Angeles River was no longer adequate for its water needs. Official eyes turned towards the Owens Valley, a remote inland area 250 miles north of Los Angeles, which benefited from a significant run-off from the Sierra Madre. At the time, the hopes of the local farmers were raised by the possibility that the Federal government might fund an irrigation project which would immensely expand the agricultural potential of the valley. The Federal government sent in an engineer from its Reclamation Service called J.B. Lippincott to make recommendations on an irrigation project. What Lippincott failed to tell local farmers was that he was also a consulting engineer for the Los Angeles Water Department. Lippincott was followed by a Los Angeles Water Department employee who set about buying up land needed for the construction of an aqueduct to far away Los Angeles (while noising around that he, too, was affiliated with the Federal Reclamation service.) With the vital land under its control, Los Angeles started work on the aqueduct and the local farmers found themselves robbed of their water. This unsavory piece of duplicity formed the central theme of a movie classic, Roman Polanski's "Chinatown," the 1975 Oscar winner, and the renown of that film will ensure that what became known the "Owens Valley Land Grab" will never be forgotten.

Los Angeles had to wait for another century to experience a similar act of official sleaze. This time it was the turn of the Los Angeles County Board of Supervisors, a five-man outfit which governs the wealthiest county in the whole of the United States. Soon after the Second World War the Federal government approved a project to convert part of a swampy wetland on Los Angeles' west coast into a marina to be called Marina del Rey. As it was originally conceived the Marina was to be a huge recreational park for Los Angeles' west side providing docks and boating facilities for 6,000 small craft. The issue of funding the Marina construction was put before voters in 1956. It contained the proviso that the County could repay its revenue bonds by awarding leases to apartment builders, hotels and restaurants for a strictly limited period of 60 years. But once the developers' appetites were whetted for the rich pickings of this prime ocean side site there was no looking back. And they were aided and abetted by County Supervisors who saw the Marina as a convenient cash provider.

The story of how the private developers' Marina to a large extent swallowed the recreational Marina (and my own involvement in these goings on) is the subject of this book.

CHAPTER TWO

Mother's Beach

It was a constant source of astonishment to me that an organization like Reuters News Agency which deals exclusively in the dissemination of hard facts should, at its administrative level, be so prone to rumor and leaks. Employed by the agency since 1954, I had been back at London headquarters cooling my heels in 1968 while waiting to be told of my new assignment when a secretary called me aside and confided: "They're sending you to Los Angeles." And then to express her own surprise that a reporter with a reputation for scoring considerable scoops should be so in the dark about his own future, she added: "Didn't you know?"

Most of my years with Reuters had been spent covering trouble spots in Asia and Africa. Los Angeles, although scarcely a trouble spot, was nevertheless a pioneer posting for the agency so my reputation for using my initiative in the field played into my being given this assignment. In its nearly a century-and-a-half of existence, Reuters had never had a correspondent in that southern California metropolis. It got most of its United States news in an exchange agreement with the Associated Press. In the sixties the Associated Press chose to end this agreement and Reuters had to scramble to cover the United States from its own resources.

My journalistic career had started back in my native Australia working for the *Adelaide Advertiser* and *Melbourne Herald*, both owned by Sir Keith Murdoch, father of the internationally much better known, Rupert Murdoch. But Australians inevitably yearn for seeing the world beyond their tight big island and in 1953 I set off for Canada aboard a freighter to explore the Americas. From Vancouver in British Columbia there was only one way to go — South. So I went south and I kept going south. I thumbed my way three times back and forth across the United States taking in virtually every state, down through Mexico and Central America, into Colombia aboard an extraordinary Indian wooden craft, through the jungles of a Colombia which was being torn by a brutal civil war, and thence to Peru and across the jungles of the Brazilian interior to end up in Carnival in Rio in 1954.

Landing in London in 1954 I used my journalist's credentials and references from the Murdoch organization to get a summer relief job at Reuters. The following year I was hired permanently by Reuters and set off on my first assignment in Asia, which, after several diversions mid-course, turned out to be Thailand. That country had been under the thumb of a dapper little dictator called Pibulsonggram since the days of Japanese occupation in the Second World War but his authority was being increasingly contested by the Army. One night, sensing that something was afoot, I jumped in my car and headed for the center of Bangkok to find tanks sitting athwart many of the city intersections. I headed for the post office to send off a brief flash: "TANKS APPEARED IN CENTRAL BANGKOK LATE TONIGHT AS THE ARMY MOVED IN TO TAKE OVER." It was a considerable scoop over the opposition and through it I acquired my reputation of being the go-to guy for covering trouble spots.

I have always adhered to the firm rule that a foreign correspondent is no better than his local tipsters and in Bangkok I had the local help of a burly Thai of Chinese ancestry called The. While the opposition agencies floundered in the confusion of the aftermath of the Army coup, through my local help I got it all right. I named the Army nominee who was to head the new government and on the fate of the deposed Pibulsonggram I was right on the button. Opposition agencies had him fleeing to neighboring Burma and Malaya, but I reported: "PIBULSONGGRAM IS HEADED FOR CAMBODIA IN A WHITE FORD THUNDERBIRD."

After Thailand I reported on the revolt of the colonels against the dictatorial rule of President Sukarno, sending dispatches on interviews with the rebel colonels in the three regions of Sumatra which were probably as closely read by authorities in Djakarta as by Reuters subscribers. I covered the mainland Chinese shelling of the Nationalist-held islands of Quemoy and Matsu, scrambling ashore from a navy craft as the shells poured in. I travelled with Presidents Ho Chi Minh of Vietnam and Marshall Tito on their tours of the Indonesian islands. I covered the 1960 coup attempt against President Ngo Dinh Diem. My exclusive dispatch saying Diem had refused to yield to the rebels surrounding his palace as they were claiming, actually played a role in the outcome of the attempted coup, as army forces loyal to the President in the delta region of the south-west heard the dispatch broadcast over Radio Manila and moved in with tanks to crush the rebellion. (Once again this scoop was owed to a first-rate local tipster or stringer as they are called in the profession. Name of Pham Xuan An. He later turned out to be a colonel in the employ of the Vietcong secret service but I still maintain he was a bloody good legman.) I covered the overthrow of the United States-backed government in Laos by a little Army captain called Kong Le. After all this Reuters sent me to Tokyo for three months for what I think they regarded as well-deserved rest and recreation for the years spent in remote outposts. But inevitably the coups d'etat followed me. I had scarcely got myself installed in Tokyo when South Korea' strongman Syngman Rhee was overthrown and I spent long hours backstopping the reporting of our correspondents in Seoul.

Africa followed Asia. And once again the turmoil in the Congo and other upsets in the newly minted republics of former British and French Africa.

I could scarcely expect Los Angeles and California to provide the coups and revolts of Asia and Africa. But what happened during my ten years there probably got much more worldwide attention than anything I had reported on from those two continents. Foremost among these events was the assassination of Senator Robert Kennedy. But just as big was the arrest and trial of self-appointed hippie guru Charles Manson and his acolytes for the murder of film actress Sharon Tate and her friends.

In fact Los Angeles in the later sixties and the seventies turned out to be a bubbling cauldron of news events. On one morning I threaded my way through supertight security at the Los Angeles courthouse to cover the arraignment of Sirhan Sirhan for the murder of Senator Robert Kennedy after spending much of the night before reporting on the drug overdose death of rocker Janice Joplin. I raced to the courthouse one day to get there just in time to hear Susan Atkins confess to the murder of Sharon Tate after having been shaken out of my bed that very morning by a major earthquake in the Los Angeles basin. I covered the endless months of the Manson trial, the Ellsberg trial (for leaking confidential Vietnam War documents), the Angela Davis trial (for providing the guns used in a bloody courtroom takeover) and the Patty Hearst trial (for participating in an armed bank raid while kidnap victim of a radical underground group). And on one memorable day I stood outside a courtroom in the Santa Monica courthouse as reporters were told that Roman Polanski had fled the country rather than continue to attend his trial for sex with a thirteen-year-old girl. The director famed for movies with a bizarre touch such as "Rosemary's Baby" and "Chinatown" had in fact created a "Chinatown" of his own, of socially proscribed sex, bringing to a halt a brilliant Hollywood career.

Celebrity news was, of course, a major part of the assignment. I stood alongside Marlon Brando on a grassy knoll atop the Santa Monica Mountains as he gave his land back to the Indians. I covered the return of Charlie Chaplin to Hollywood after his long years in exile. I spent a good hour at Los Angeles airport chewing the fat with legendary singer Louis Armstrong as he waited for friends to pick him up. And — one more trial — I reported on the Aspen, Colorado trial of French singer Claudine Longet (Mrs Andy Williams) for the shooting death of her ski star lover Spider Sabich. I raced gingerly across an ice-covered road to report on the verdict on a phone which I had installed in the basement of a church. But there was no time for hanging around after filing this report. I had to dash for a plane to Utah to cover the execution of Gary Gilmore for the murder of gas station attendants. This was a major event because it represented a return to the death penalty in the United States after fifteen years in legal abeyance. Gilmore's story was chronicled in the Norman Mailer book "The Executioner's Song." Prison authorities had arranged for the installation of phones for my competitors of AP and UPI but had failed to provide for my request for a Reuters phone. The prison governor very graciously allowed me to use his office and phone and from there I reported that Gilmore in his last hours was dancing the tango with his aunt in his cell and also his ultimate dispatch at the hands of a firing squad.

In my ten years of reporting on Los Angeles I struck up friendships with some pretty remarkable colleagues. Among them was the doyenne of celebrity trial reporting, Theo Wilson, and her successor to that title, Linda Deutsch of Associated Press. Also Ivor Davis, correspondent for the British *Daily Express,* who had come to the United States reporting on a Beatles tour, and had decided that Los Angeles was the spot for him. But perhaps the most remarkable of all was Mary Neiswender, reporter for a Los Angeles area newspaper, who had a penchant for going off quietly to arrange exclusive access to major criminals, while the rest of us were tied down on press conferences with prosecution and defence attorneys. Incredibly, Mary pulled this off with the most notorious criminal of them all. She became the exclusive channel for statements from Charles Manson. The only downside of this, she tells me, was when her newspaper patched Manson's calls through to her home and her blood would run cold as her teenage daughter shouted "Mom, it's Charlie" or "Mom, it's Charlie again." But she says Manson was a long way from being the most evil of the killers who confided in her. Anyone who chooses to read her book with the lengthy title "Assassins...Serial Killers... Corrupt Cops...Chasing the News in a Skirt and High Heels" must be prepared for some pretty gut-churning accounts of serial killers who tortured to death young girls and young boys.

The Los Angeles assignment came to an end in 1978 with my appointment as Reuters bureau chief in Washington. I spent 13 years there but this world of congressional debate, diplomacy and government regulation was never as much fun as the glitzy scene of Los Angeles.

And at the end of the 13 years in Washington, RETIREMENT. But where? That was the question.

I went back to my birthplace of Adelaide, Australia, a peaceful and very livable city well away from the hectic metropolises of Sydney and Melbourne. "We would love to have you back," my relatives told me. "But you'd have to learn to play bridge."

No way.

A second choice was my wife's native land of France. But it eventually proved to be unsuitably remote from our affairs in the United States.

So it was back to the United States itself. Not Washington. Thirteen years there was quite enough. We looked at Florida but that seemed to me to have a mortuary touch compared to the lively world of Los Angeles.

So Los Angeles it was. We moved into a condominium in the Pacific Ocean neighborhood of Marina del Rey.

And that was how it all started.

Almost every day my constitutional walks would take me past the picnic tables and sandy children's playground of Mother's Beach. At weekends and on public holidays the picnic tables were full with family parties from all over the Los Angeles basin. The area was a babel of the languages of the various migrant families. The air was scented with the smells of ethnic cooking coming from the barbecues. On the north side of the beach colorful rowing boats, outriggers and kayaks were drawn up on the sand and children set out from this safe launch pad in their rubber dinghies. It was a colorful sight which would have delighted the French impressionist painters. Mother's Beach was the living center of the Marina, a Marina which was being rapidly overrun by strip apartment blocks.

And then I heard the astonishing news. Los Angeles County was planning to shut down the picnic tables of Mother's Beach and push picnic families over to the other side of the Marina where there was no sand for their children to play. It also planned to transfer the non-powered boat launch to an unsafe deep-water launch on the other side of the Marina.

I was horrified. I was also prodded into action.

The one eventuality I had never thought of when I took my retirement was that I might become involved in civic activism. But closing down Mother's Beach. That was too much.

I got involved.

CHAPTER THREE

"Who is the Man Up There?"

The city of Santa Monica, with its high bluffs overlooking the gleaming expanse of the Pacific Ocean, is one of the main terminuses in southern California of the American rush towards the west. It is the final point of Highway 66, the legendary road which linked the eastern part of the country with the Californian coast. A pier in Santa Monica was the original port for passengers and cargo entering the Los Angeles area, a pier that has long-since vanished and been replaced by the mega-ports of San Pedro and Long Beach. Today its principal attraction is as a leisure destination for Los Angeles residents seeking escape from the inland summer heat and of vacationers from all over the country and the world.

Santa Monica is also the center point in the long-running controversy of citizens' access to the beach. To the north is the city of Malibu which is largely off-limits for beach-goers apart from an occasional strip or niche of sand. Houses built abutting each other form a wall for miles and miles blocking off the beach. Attempts to open up access meet with the most determined opposition from property owners, sworn to defend their private beach down to the last legal brief. The situation is further complicated by California's wacko coastal laws. Instead of declaring all sand in the public domain as in Oregon, California sets a divider of the mean high tide line — whatever that may mean. The ocean side of this constantly-changing line drawn in the sand is in public domain, the other side belongs to beachside property owners. If a beachgoer who manages to find a way through the wall of housing strays too far toward the dunes he or she is likely to be warned off by scooter-borne patrols employed by the house owners. Or suffer the fate of a Boston rabbi and his family who were driven off at gunpoint by bushy-bearded screen actor Steve McQueen.

Santa Monica and beaches to the south are not involved in this idiotic policy of the mean high tide line. Their beaches are completely open to the public and for decades they have been a favored venue for leisure seekers from all over the Los Angeles basin. To the south is Ocean Park, now a part of Santa Monica, and further south is Venice, since 1925 incorporated within the city of Los Angeles. These two areas have a vibrant history of being the fun fair of greater Los Angeles.

Anyone who wanders through the run-down alleys of present day Venice is likely to be confronted by two enormous portraits painted on the brick walls. One of these is easily recognized. It is a portrait of the rock singer Jim Morrison of the Doors, a lousy poet and the singer of a number of successful songs, who died of a drug overdose in a Paris hotel and is interred in Paris' resting place of the famous, the Pere Lachaise cemetery. The second portrait is more of a puzzle. I overheard a little girl ask her mother, "Mommy, who is the man up there?" The "man" is Abbot Kinney, and whereas Jim Morrison probably had nothing to do with Venice apart from being an icon for the drug-oriented lifestyle of its rougher quarters, Abbot Kinney had everything to do with that city.

A tobacco mogul who settled in Santa Monica after touring much of the world, he saw the opportunities of the beaches to the south. He formed a partnership to build amusement parks in Ocean Park, immediately to the south of Santa Monica, and when that partnership split up, he opted to take over the swamplands to the south of Ocean Park. There Abbot Kinney revealed himself as a true visionary. He decided to build a city modeled on the Venice of Renaissance Italy with the hopes of spurring a renaissance in American and particularly Californian culture. He borrowed the name of the city of his inspiration. His creation was called the City of Venice. His workmen dug out miles of canals, watered by a wide main canal. He built columned arcades and a Bridge of Sighs. The principal hotel was the Hotel Saint Mark. And as a final touch he imported two dozen gondolas and gondoliers from Venice to offer boat rides to visitors. The Venice of his dreams was originally wildly successful. 40,000 people showed up for the city's dedication on the United States national holiday of July the Fourth in 1905.

But if Abbot Kinney was a man of many talents — he was a linguist, botanist and a connoisseur of art among other things — engineering was not one of them. His canals, hastily dug to meet his pressing development timetable, were scooped out in the course of a single winter. They were shallow and no work was done on the canal floors. Tidal action was insufficient to maintain water circulation through eight miles of these shallow ditches and they became smelly and were eventually condemned as a menace to public health. The fortunes of Venice's huge amusement park with its roller coaster, bungee-style drops and a monster swimming pool able to accommodate 2,000 bathers began to decline. Its canal-side homes which had originally housed the likes of movie idols Janet Gaynor, Norma Shearer, Harold Lloyd and movie cowboy William S. Hart, lost their luster. In 1925 Venice was annexed to the city of Los Angeles which had no interest in pouring money into restoring its network of canals. In 1929 after years of court battles Los Angeles paved over most of the canals, including the central lagoon, and the Venice ocean front was set on its urban slide towards the promenade of marijuana shops, nose-piercing and tattoo parlors which it is today. Only in one quadrant of the original Kinney grid did the city keep the original waterways. Paradoxically this small area of five canals has not only survived the downturn of Venice's fortunes but has become one of the most sought-after real estate patches of Los Angeles. Architect-designed homes have sprung up along its canals and its houses provide an exciting garden stroll for visitors who manage to find their way into this neighborhood hidden away between the busy thoroughfares of Venice.

Abbot Kinney died in November 1920. And as if to mark the passing of this man of vision, a month later a gas heater set fire to curtains in the Venice dance pavilion and the entire wooden pier of his Playland of the Pacific with its many carnival attractions went up in flames in a Wagnerian Valhalla-like conflagration. One other thing died with him. And that was any vestige of imagination in the development of Los Angeles' western beaches.

The fun fairs survived for several decades on the piers of Ocean Park and the restored attractions of Venice but they were eventually abandoned and torn down. A new form of family entertainment had entered the scene. The beach playlands had up to this point formed an entirely separate development from Los Angeles' other entertainment industry — the movie studios of Hollywood. But in the 1960's the two concepts came together. Some thirty miles inland in the city of Anaheim, the Magical Kingdom of Disneyland opened its doors.

CHAPTER FOUR

"I Dug a Ditch (U.S.) I Struck it Rich (L.A. County)"

As the fun fairs on west Los Angeles beaches declined in popularity, attention was turned to the undeveloped area directly to the south of Venice — the wetlands of the Ballona Creek estuary.

Activity had always been on a big scale in this scrubby wasteland with its meandering waterways and inner lagoon. Around 1820 a Mexican rancher called Agostino Machado got a land grant from the Mexican government to graze his cattle on 14,000 acres stretching well inland from the estuary. He called his land "Rancho La Ballona." But with California changing ownership in the U.S.-Mexico war of 1847 Machado lost his claim to the land. Next on the scene was a developer who drew up ambitious plans to found a community called Ballona Village on the northern rim of the wetlands in the 1880's. He began dredging a harbor and a canal between the ocean and the inland lagoon and a railway line was laid into the site of the village in 1887. But despite all of this preparatory activity, the project never got off the ground and Ballona Village remained only a concept on paper.

In the nineteen hundreds, the Ballona wetlands became the property of industrialist and aviator Howard Hughes. In a factory set inland from the maze of waterways of the estuary he built his huge wooden transport plane called the Spruce Goose with the idea of helping in America's war effort against Japan. Hughes was an eccentric character from the outset but at the end of his life he became a psychotic recluse, lying curled up naked in his private sanctum, letting his hair and fingernails grow uncut, and even preserving his urine and feces in jars around him. His death in 1976 must have been followed by one gargantuan toilet flush. His heirs and officials of his Summa corporation drew up plans to develop a community called Playa del Vista (today Playa Vista) consuming most of the 1,187 acres of the wetlands. This scheme drew the fierce opposition of ecologists who wanted to preserve the natural beauties and bird sanctuaries of the wetlands, and eventually the Hughes group sold the area to another developer who agreed to preserve a large portion of the wetlands and pay for much of their restoration.

In 1936 the question of what to do with the Ballona wetlands once more came to the fore in a hearing held in Venice by the U.S. Army Corps of Engineers. A number of different opinions were advanced by the 123 interested parties attending as to what exactly the wetlands were to become. Congressman Leland Ford expressed the hope that the area could become like San Francisco's Golden Gate park for the people of Los Angeles.

Los Angeles County Board of Supervisors was given the job of drawing up a plan for developing the wetlands and suggesting how it should be funded. It is in the title of their report that the name "Marina del Rey" initially appears and Marina del Rey it was to become. Their preliminary design envisioned an inner lagoon and entrance channel comprising 646 acres of waterways with moorings for about 5,200 small boats. In order for the plan to win favor with the non-boating public, the report placed emphasis on the general recreational activities the Marina could provide including bathing, picnicking and athletics. Several significant changes were made in decisions of local authorities and the Corps of Engineers which included eliminating the central lagoon concept and replacing it with a straight main channel with seven moles. The Corps of Engineers redesign increased the number of mooring slips to 6,200.

Marina del Rey finally became a reality in 1954 when President Eisenhower signed a bill under which the Federal government agreed to pay half the cost of its construction.

The County of Los Angeles was faced with a critical choice on how to pay for its part of the development. Funding the work through general obligation bonds repayable solely on the good credit of the County would have required a two thirds vote of the local electorate. Revenue bonds, on the other hand, were backed by moneys gained from leasing part of the area to developers, and these required the approval of only 50 per cent of voters. The County opted for the second scheme and although the decision seemed an understandable one at the time (the voters approved the measure by a two to one margin) it had serious long term consequences. In effect, from that point, the concept of Marina del Rey as a huge public park serving the citizens of western Los Angeles had been significantly modified.

The County set up a number of organizations to manage the development of the Marina. These included a Design Control Board given authority over reviewing projects and enforcing architectural standards.

However the County ran into leasing problems which it had not initially anticipated. There was much less competition for leases than they had expected, with only three of the 13 parcels finally leased getting more than one bid.

This raised concerns among bondholders as to whether there would be money available to repay their bonds, and to meet their concerns the County decided to make several major concessions in the terms of their leases.

The County's actions resulted in a further drift away from the initial concept of the Marina as a predominantly leisure venue by placing the emphasis on more intensive development of high-revenue residential and commercial developments.

Its new leasing policies were eventually to make the County the target of accusations about favoritism in its lease awards and alleged "give-away deals."

CHAPTER FIVE

"Go directly to jail.
Do not pass GO."

The opening salvo directed against the County's management of the Marina was fired by reporter Jack Keating of the now-defunct *Los Angeles Herald-Express* who charged the County was involved in 'give-away deals'.

He specifically questioned whether favored parties were receiving special treatment in the allocation of Marina del Rey concessions. He noted that only three of the 13 parcels leased at the Marina at that time received more than one bid, while neighboring yacht harbors on the California coastline had received multiple bids in virtually every concession category. Keating said that Marina officials blamed the poor bidding on the fact that county rules forbade the use of county general funds or harbor bond revenues for publicizing the bidding process. But he charged that the Board of Supervisors was taking advantage of these restrictions to make it easier to award contracts to the developers they favored.

The Keating article stirred the supervisors to clean up their leasing processes. A "watchdog committee" was set up to keep an eye on leasing decisions and a rule was introduced making it obligatory to have more than one bid on any concession.

But if the County thought it had brought an end to Marina del Rey-based controversy with these clean-up decisions it was soon to learn otherwise. In fact the County's management of the Marina during the first phase was marked by one crisis after another.

The region's primary newspaper, the *Los Angeles Times* and a beachside giveaway weekly, *The Argonaut*, followed up on the enquiries set in motion by the *Herald-Express*.

At the height of a bitterly contested election in 1980 for the Fourth Supervisorial district of the County Board of Supervisors, *The Argonaut* reported on a speech of one of the candidates, Yvonne Braithwaite Burke, saying that if her opponent was elected it would lead to 'corruption of the Board of Supervisors by developers.'

Noting that the Marina constituted the biggest profit-making enterprise the County had, she asked: "Is the Marina a recreational resource or is it a business resource?" She promised that if elected she would fight to keep Marina Fund moneys in the Marina, rather than support other supervisors who sought to divert these revenues into the county's general fund.

Yvonne Burke lost and the Marina moneys were promptly swept into the general fund for use on a multitude of county-wide projects with a very limited amount being turned back for the upkeep of the Marina.

Times reporter Jeffrey Rabin, in a 1989 three-part series entitled "The Ties are Cozy" revealed that the Marina's biggest property owner Abe Lurie was delinquent on a million dollars in property taxes for the previous year and that private lenders had declared him in default on a further million dollars in loans. Lurie's annual property taxes amounted to $3.3 million dollars, about a fifth of the County's revenue from the Marina at that time.

This was the last thing the Board of Supervisors wanted to hear. They feared that if Lurie went bankrupt it could undermine their entire Marina operation resulting in further millions of dollars in lost revenue. Added to that, Lurie was a major political contributor in Los Angeles County. Their first reaction was to turn a blind eye towards Lurie's business operations. The director of its Beaches and Harbors department declared, "I have never been aware he was having these sort of problems."

The situation was dire. Lurie owned at least four hotels in the Marina, apartment houses, offices, restaurants, shops and boat slips. But a rescuer was already on the scene promising a major cash infusion in exchange for 49.9 per cent of Lurie's properties. The only problem was that Lurie refused to reveal publicly who the investor was and the county counsel warned that the County could face problems under federal anti-racketeering statutes if tainted money was invested in the Marina. Outside counsel advised the County to seek specific financial guarantees from the investors, but, pressured by Lurie's lobbying, they finally agreed to the transaction on the basis of a letter from the investor's Chicago attorney that his clients' businesses "did not in any way involve trafficking in drugs, laundering money or other criminal activity."

The secret investors turned out to be a Middle-Eastern group headed by billionaire Saudi Arabian businessman and arms brokers Khalid and Abdul Aziz Al-Ibrahim, brothers-in-law of King Saud.

Abe Lurie's problems were largely brought on by his over-investment in hotels. Despite being over-extended, he embarked in the late sixties on the construction of a nine-story hotel, the Marina Plaza. Lurie dug a hole on the lot and poured the hotel's cement foundations, possibly to preserve his claim on the site. Yet 15 years after work started the hotel had still not been built and

Los Angeles County, which had been very patient up to this point, voted in 1983 to extend his long term lease if he would proceed promptly with building the hotel. The Marina Plaza has not been built to this day. The abandoned site with its ugly cement-filled hole has been a constant source of embarrassment to the County. And in the meantime, to complicate matters further, the Army Corps of Engineers stepped in to declare the often water-logged hole a protected wetland, in effect turning the fenced-in plot over to the birds.

Lurie's troubles with the Marina Plaza and another hotel, the Marina Beach Hotel which had failed to make a profit from the moment of his opening, caused him to turn back to the investors who had rescued him in the first place. According to a 1991 *Los Angeles Times* article by the same author Jeffrey Rabin, Lurie agreed in October 1990 to sell the rest of his Marina holdings to the Saudis for $15.3 million with the Saudis also agreeing to assume more than $130 million in debts on the properties. The deal would have ensured Lurie remaining on as a managing partner but in June 1991 the Saudis lost their stomach for the deal and they filed a suit in Los Angeles Superior Court seeking to dissolve the partnership and accusing Lurie of engaging in 'fraud and abuse.'

Lurie filed for bankruptcy. The Saudis filed their own reorganization plan for the Marina properties which involved them becoming the sole owner of Lurie's holdings and they eventually ended up controlling the largest bloc of his properties, according to a *Times* article by Rabin and reporter Ron Russell.

However the Saudi investors turned out to be as problematical for the County as Lurie had been. In 1997 the same *Los Angeles Times* reporting team revealed that the Middle Eastern businessman who had bought most of Lurie's properties had himself filed for bankruptcy. The County succeeded in removing six properties from the bankruptcy proceedings and transferred leases on hundreds of boats slips, an apartment complex, shopping centers, restaurants and offices to a Boston-based owner.

While the decline and fall of Abe Lurie was playing out, another major crisis was brewing in the Marina. Apartment tenants, boat slip renters and liveaboards had become concerned with rapid increases in their rents spurred by the end of rent control and they cast around for a way of ending what they regarded as rent gouging. Their answer was to seek cityhood for the Marina enclave which would put them in the driver's seat on matters such as rent increases. The Marina renters were encouraged by the success of a similar cityhood drive in West Hollywood, center of Los Angeles' largest gay community. That community felt that the Los Angeles County government showed insufficient understanding and support for their particular lifestyle and in 1984 they sued for incorporation as an autonomous city and won. But if the Los Angeles Board of Supervisors was willing to let West Hollywood go without putting up a battle, Marina del Rey was a very different matter. The Marina was producing revenue for the County general fund. The County promptly began a major lobbying effort in the State capital of Sacramento to block the breakaway move. They were aided by Marina lessees who feared a renter-dominated administration might re-impose rent controls. In 1985 they got a bill introduced in the State senate which would block cityhood for areas where less than 50 per cent of the land was privately owned. The bill did not specifically mention Marina del Rey but this was practically the only area throughout the State where the restrictions of the bill could apply. The lessees first enlisted Senator William Lockyer, a Democrat from the northern city of Hayward, to sponsor the bill but Lockyer got into difficulty in his own constituency over the terms of the bill, and he dropped out. To take his place the County and lessees turned to Senator Joseph Montoya of the southern California City of Whittier. Getting Montoya's help to sponsor bills, as it subsequently turned out, could be a rather expensive business. Montoya got the bill passed by a narrow majority but his own term in the Senate was drawing to an unsavory close. The Federal Bureau of Investigation, alerted by Montoya's suspect readiness to support an unusual number of legislative proposals, mounted a sting operation directed at his office. They set up a fake shrimp packaging company and taped a meeting with Montoya at which the State senator asked for $3,000 for his supporting vote. Montoya went on trial and was found guilty of seven of 10 counts of racketeering, extortion and money laundering. Montoya's support of Los Angeles County and its Marina lessees was not an issue in the trial and it is not known if he attempted to extort money from these two organizations.

But the rapidly expanding net of the FBI against influence peddling brought the whole issue much closer to the Marina. In November 1991 Federal authorities filed racketeering charges against powerful State Senator Alan Robbins, accusing him of extorting money from special interests, engaging in obstruction of justice and filing a false tax return. Robbins, who was a partner with one of the Marina's most influential families of developers in the ownership of two large apartment blocks, boat slips and restaurants, admitted to the charges and immediately resigned his State office. He received a 4 ½ year prison sentence and a heavy fine. The sentence was later reduced by his agreeing to act as an FBI front in another sting. Robbins' Marina dealings were not part of the Federal charges but the Robbins scandal once again brought the Marina under unfavorable public scrutiny, attention the County would have dearly liked to do without.

The final prison sentence linked to the Marina arose from a very sad affair.

For decades the dapper figure of lawyer Richard Fine, clad in business suit and butterfly tie, had been seen around the Los Angeles courthouses defending the rights of citizens against official abuse. One of his main campaigns was directed against Los Angeles County judges who received a large annual booster to their State salary from the County which made them better paid than even the justices of the United States Supreme Court. Fine argued that these large bonuses made it unlikely that the judges would rule against the County in any court case in which the County was involved. He called the payments 'bribes' and raised issues about whether the judges were reporting the payments properly in their tax returns.

Fine's fundamental error was probably taking on too many causes, thereby making a string of powerful enemies. He entered the Marina fray, taking on the case of neighbors of an apartment complex named Del Rey Shores who objected the size and residential density of the development. They were eagerly backed by many tenants of The Shores who objected to being thrown out of their apartments so that the developers could tear down their 202-low level garden-like complex and replace it with 544 luxury apartments. Fine charged that two of the County supervisors who approved a critical permit for rebuilding the apartment block had received political donations from the developer and his associates within six weeks of their vote of approval and were in violation of the California Political Reform Act which forbade political contributions being given and votes being cast within a specified time frame.

The judge assigned to the case was David Yaffe. Fine opened up with a broadside of charges calling on him to withdraw from hearing the case. The charges included that Yaffe had received $230,000 in payments from Los Angeles County which was a party to the case and that he had failed to report the payments as required by the Political Reform Act. The judge countered by charging that Fine had "attacked the integrity of the Los Angeles Superior Court" and, in a most unusual proceeding, appeared as witness in the trial of Fine in which he was sitting as judge. Fine misstepped in filing an appeal in the Del Rey Shores case one day late and in order not to prejudice his clients' rights to proceed, he filed an affidavit which made him liable for reasonable costs and fees. On January 8, 2008, Judge Yaffe held a hearing in which he ordered Fine to pay sanctions and Del Rey Shores attorneys' fees of $47,000. Fine, who by that time, had been stripped of his right to practice law by a committee of his fellow lawyers and no longer represented the Del Rey Shores neighbors, held that he had not been notified of the hearing and refused to cooperate with the committee which would determine the actual amount he owed and how it should be paid. The judge found him in contempt of court and sentenced him to indefinite solitary confinement in a Los Angeles jail until he cooperated with the committee.

During my time as a reporter in Los Angeles I had been witness to similar coercive action by a judge in which one of my reporter colleagues, Bill Farr of the *Los Angeles Times*, was sentenced to jail until he revealed the source of a story about the Manson trial. With others of my reporter group I visited Farr in jail to keep his spirits up. But Farr had been jailed under a California law which limited the extent of such coercive imprisonment to five days if it became clear he would continue to refuse to comply. Judge Yaffe had sentenced Fine under another section which permitted indefinite imprisonment where defendants refused "to perform an act which is yet in the power of the person to perform." In other words Judge Yaffe was ready to see Fine rot in solitary confinement unless he complied with the court order.

Richard Fine was confined to a small, windowless cell in Los Angeles County Men's Central Jail with no warrant issued for his arrest, and no court judgment, conviction or sentencing ever entered in his case. No valid booking records were ever found for his arrest and confinement. The Los Angeles County Sheriff insisted he had been jailed on the authority of the "Municipal Court of San Pedro." Problem — no such court exists.

"Free Richard Fine" movements sprang up in Fine's defense. But in this age of the Blog there were others who argued that Fine's wounds were self-inflicted and that the whole matter revealed the "sad state of Mr. Fine's psychiatric functioning." What these people failed to take into account was that in almost every instance Fine was proved right. In February 2009 the California State Governor Arnold Schwartzenegger, known as The Gubernator for his movie roles as the Terminator, signed a 'retroactive immunities bill' covering the operations of Los Angeles County judges, the sort of measure usually used to cover some specific wrongdoing. Fine supporters swiftly dubbed it a 'pardon' of the judges.

Eventually Judge Yaffe, upon his retirement from the bench, did free Fine, stating ungraciously that any man who put up with a year and a half in prison rather than comply with a simple court order was clearly of unsound mind.

For Los Angeles County the Fine affair came at the end of fifty chaotic years of its Marina administration during which its operations had often been subjected to unwelcome press coverage. With the disposition of large additional areas in the Marina coming up for decision, County officials were obviously intent on finding a better and less contentious way of doing business. One County official pointed out that Los Angeles was running a unique operation for an elective municipal body. Part of it was the usual role of providing public services such as roads, libraries etc. The other part of it was managing the Marina which he saw as a business operation. Businesses, he said, were entitled to use secrecy in pursuit of their profit goals and he felt Los Angeles County was entitled to the same sort of secrecy in its Marina operations.

The County also decided to use a second tool of big business in its Marina operations — that was the use of public relations resources to put a 'spin', or favorable light, on its operations.

But the County might have been forewarned that the use of secrecy by an elective body can give rise to arrogance and a complete disregard of public interests. And the diversion of resources to 'spin', if taken too far, can cause the same elective body to stray over the danger line into outright lying.

CHAPTER SIX

The Five Little Kings

The Board of Supervisors which governs the County of Los Angeles has created a most curious décor for its deliberations. Instead of the parliamentary pit favored by most deliberative bodies with spectators seated in galleries, the five elected supervisors themselves occupy the gallery looking down on the members of the public far below. The effect is rather like a setting for a Greek tragedy with the gods occupying the high ground and the lower level being reserved for mere mortals. As it happens, the attitudes of the supervisors can often seem godlike — ranging from sublime indifference to the goings on below — one supervisor has a habit of reading his newspaper during deliberations — to a gaze of smiling condescension for the supplications of the mortals below. And occasionally the gods can turn angry, showering down the thunderbolts of their wrath on citizens they think have overstepped the proper bounds of protest and signaling their displeasure to County marshals who haul the offenders up out of their seats, pin their hands behind their backs and march them off into detention.

Newspapers have dubbed the supervisors 'the Five Little Kings' (an appellation that sticks despite the fact there is often a queen or two). And in truth they have almost a regal sway over the ten million citizens of Los Angeles County, a fifth of whom live in unincorporated cities within the county boundaries and fall directly under their administration. Their budget is huge — 24.7 billion dollars in a recent year. Besides their salary, each supervisor is accorded an annual grant of 3.4 million dollars to spend on office luxuries and pet projects. Their territory stretches from the Pacific Ocean to the desert and to wild mountain ranges where straying hikers can end up dying of hunger and exposure. Their electorates are cobbled together from bits and pieces of territory sometimes with the aim of favoring this or that ethnic group and thus going beyond the political practice of gerrymandering, or shaping electoral districts to favor one party or another. That political ploy was named in part for a Massachusetts governor called Jerry and partly after the salamander whose shape one of his districts was said to resemble. Governor Jerry's district was at least one contiguous area, even if weirdly shaped, but some Los Angeles supervisorial districts are cobbled together from pieces all over the shop. The result is that most Los Angeles citizens have an incomplete and confused picture of the functioning of their county government and turn out for county elections rarely reaches twenty five per cent. This minimal public interest ensures the reelection of incumbent supervisors, once electable any number of times but since 2002 restricted to three, four-year terms.

My first encounter with the doings of the Los Angeles Board of Supervisors gave me the impression that this was a very odd electoral body indeed. In the opening section of their deliberations, the supervisors droned on with testimonials to citizens who had died within the preceding week. This was followed by the issuing of plaques and certificates of merit to various citizens groups. One supervisor took the microphone hugging a little dog and pleading for animal adoption. Decisions on motions before the board seemed to me to be decided in advance with the Supervisors voting down the line on recommendations put to them by their staff.

The first board meeting I attended also produced one small incident which I found disconcerting. A number of small foster home operations which had failed to file for the extension of their contracts in time were told by the Board chair that if they had failed to meet the filing deadline there was nothing the County could do about it. A few moments later, a colleague of mine told the supervisors that a developer in Marina del Rey had not only failed to meet his finishing date on construction of a large block of apartments but he had not even started building. This contractor later had his lease extended for four years in return for a payment of one million dollars.

On most issues, members of the public are given three minutes to express their views but this can be cut to a mere one minute if there is a big turn out. Any citizen who exceeds the appointed time limit is abruptly cut off. For most citizens this chance to address the supervisors is a once-in-a-lifetime event but one Los Angeleno has made it a once-a-week commitment.

Los Angeles media have dubbed citizen Eric Preven the "County gadfly" which is a little unfair for a man who spends so much time working to ensure County transparency and accountability but it is undoubtedly the way the Supervisors see him. After one Supervisor lost his temper with Preven's constant interventions the board voted to limit him to a total of three minutes on all issues on which he wished to speak in General Public Comment.

A former television script writer, Preven became interested in the workings of County government when he tried to get his mother's dogs released from a County pound and found it a thoroughly frustrating experience. With all the time he was spending in County hall getting the dogs sprung he became fascinated by the way the Supervisors worked and he began tracking their decisions issue by issue. Every Tuesday he turned up at the Supervisors' meeting trundling a roller laden with research he had done on motions before the Board. He does not limit himself to mere speech-making. He demands follow-ups from County staff and gets information put on the record.

Preven says of his time-consuming mission; "I am an expert on County government — unfortunately. People who know it takes time to deal with all these documents which are so dry think there must be something wrong with me that I am so focussed."

His insistence can lead to interesting facts being dredged up from the netherworld of County administration. He discovered that not only are the responsibilities of the five supervisors carved up into five separate jurisdictions, but County administration itself is compartmentalized into five distinct sections. This has some importance in the question of developments in Marina del Rey. With the Department of Beaches and Harbors, managers of the Marina, under the purview of the supervisor of the fourth district, it meant that decisions and actions on the Marina were being concocted in a separated backroom, a world onto itself, where interests of the public and recreation play distinct second fiddle to the demands of developers. (It is true that the supervisor of the third district also had jurisdiction over the Beaches and Harbor department, but his concerns were the beaches of Malibu, to the north).

As for myself, over the years of making occasional forays downtown to attend County board meetings, I did form a somewhat more favorable view of the Supervisors' operations than on my first exposure. Los Angeles, for all its glamorous Hollywood associations, is, in many parts a very troubled city. It seemed to me the Supervisors were, in general, working conscientiously to grapple with the city's many social problems such as its huge population of homeless, of mentally ill on the streets, of crime and punishment and of caring for abandoned and mistreated children.

But the issue that drew me downtown was Marina del Rey and here I found the Supervisors were failing miserably in their handling of this precious public asset.

The Little King in charge of Marina developments is the Supervisor for the Fourth District, Don Knabe. With Marina operations bringing in a steady flow of money into the County coffers, the other supervisors probably see little reason to challenge his management. In any case openly challenging the operations of another supervisor is not the County's way of doing things.

But Knabe could scarcely expect to win a similar immunity from press criticism. And in the new century Knabe was the Supervisor he got the most unfavorable press attention.

In 2011 *Los Angeles Times* columnist Patt Morrison raised the issue of the father-son relationship of Knabe and his son Matt, who was a lobbyist for a public relations firm, some of whose clients had financial dealings with the County. Knabe denied any implication of conflict of interest in an interview with Morrison saying "He (Matt) does his job and I do mine."

Morrison's column led to a follow up from a not altogether expected source. The news division of the Los Angeles public television station KCET called SoCal Connected has a habit of going into hiatus from time to time because of lack of funds. Investigative reporting costs money so SoCal Connected was not the most obvious source to launch an investigation into the business dealings of Knabe, father and son. Correspondent Vince Gonzales went on the air in 2012 with "an investigation into one supervisor with some interesting family ties."

Gonzales's attention was drawn to the fact that Knabe Sr. had introduced a motion to extend the leases on six golf course's run by American Golf Courses, one of the County's few lucrative operations. The lease extension was granted without any competitive bids, despite the fact that County audits had found American Golf-managed courses had "deficiencies...in financial reporting" and some of the courses owed the County thousands of dollars, Gonzales reported.

When it came to golf, Gonzales said, father-son relations were close. Matt Knabe Jr. often organized tournaments with his father. He created the Knabe Cup in his father's honor. He is partner in the powerful lobbying firm of Englander, Knabe and Allen, which represents the Knabe Golf Cup sponsor — the American Golf Corporation.

Gonzales raised a similar issue over the County granting a lease extension to another Englander-Knabe client, Modern Parking Incorporated, for operation of parking lots in Marina del Rey and on County beaches. The granting of the extended lease was strongly opposed by other parking lot operators who claimed Modern Parking had filed a flawed proposal that allowed them to underbid other companies by $300,000. Nevertheless MPI won the bid. Knabe Sr. voted for it.

Gonzales took his investigation of a County car rental contract a step further. Enterprise Rent-a-Car, an Englander-Knabe client, had been granted a $2 million dollar fleet management contract to provide and maintain 61 new cars for the County Housing authority. This time the contract was issued — purportedly — on the basis of competitive bidding. But Gonzales got hold of the list of the bidders and went round interviewing them. First on the list Eddie/ Fast Deer Bus Charter: "We are not renting cars. We do buses only." Next — Ken's Tires: "Don't even sell or lease cars." Others included handicap van dealers in faraway Ohio and Florida, car repair shops, tour bus companies, none of them licensed to sell or deliver new vehicles. On one point, Gonzales said, all of the supposed bidders were unanimous. None of them had place a bid or was even aware they were on the list." Supervisor Knabe voted in favor.

In most other U.S. states disclosure of this fraudulent bidding document would have had people holding their noses, screaming "stinking fish" and calling for resignations. But it seems to take a lot to move the Californian public. Supervisor Knabe, in an interview with Gonzales, said: "If it's not a good deal for the county...there is no way that being my son would change my vote. End of conversation."

Even so, Knabe could scarcely escape the implications of what had occurred in the Enterprise lease issue. Someone within the bowels of the County organization, prompted or unprompted, had faked a document to support a contract favored by a supervisor and his lobbyist son. Why? Was the county employee who did it simply trying to put himself or herself in the good books of the Knabes? Viewed any which way, the whole issue is a profound example of the corruption of a public process.

Gonzales kept up pressure and he won a promise from Supervisor Mike Antonovich, then chairman of the board, that an enquiry would be conducted into the matter and the board would get back quickly with what it discovered. I talked to Gonzales three months later. He told me nothing had been heard back yet from Antonovich's office. A year later I contacted KCET again. They still had received no word.

Which brings up another issue: the County's lack of public accountability when it comes to matters it would prefer to sweep under the rug.

CHAPTER SEVEN

GOO

The oil spill in Santa Barbara is probably little remembered these days, given the giant spills that have happened since, but its effect on public opinion at that time was instantaneous and enormous. In late January 1969 a Union Oil platform, six miles off one of the most affluent stretches of the California coast, began leaking black sludge on to beaches. Dramatic pictures of oil-covered seabirds were flashed around the United States and the world resulting in a horde of reporters, myself among them, descending on the scene. In Santa Barbara County a citizens' organization sprang up with the memorable title of GOO, three letters which stood for three little words that sent their message loud and clear — Get Oil Out! Protest parades are usually the purview of the underprivileged and unions. But in this case the citizens shouting slogans and carrying GOO banners were mostly very, very wealthy indeed. Once their slogan- shouting and banner-carrying was done they also had the ability of getting through on the phone to the powers that be in the State capital of Sacramento and demanding action. Drilling operations were halted almost immediately. The exasperated president of Union Oil, Fred Hartley, made the tactless comment: "I am amazed at the publicity for a few dead birds." In fact the oil spill had resulted in the death of more than 3,600 birds. That remark had the effect of putting a figurative match to the sludge spreading out from his oil platform.

Public revulsion to the destruction done by the oil spill resulted in a new era of ecological activism in California and the United States, along with the passage of many bills designed to give teeth to laws protecting the environment. In California one such bill was the California Environmental Quality Act (CEQA). The concerns of Californians about protecting their 1,100 miles of coastline were not restricted to the issue of oil drilling. Citizens were also worried about the large number of planned private housing and mall developments along the coast which they feared might restrict access to beaches. Citizens groups descended on the California legislature demanding the creation of a body which could control this over development. They became increasingly frustrated as their efforts to get legislation passed met with failure year after year. The California Senate is noted for being the graveyard of citizens' initiatives. Vested interests within its ranks have a way of killing reform measures in committee or letting the legislative year run out so that the slow-moving passage of legislation has to begin all over again. But in this case the obstructionist senators failed to recognize that they were dealing with a citizens' movement of tsunami proportions. California voters have an alternative method of getting the legislation they want. This is the referendum which allows for measures which garner enough signatures to be put on the ballot. In late 1972, after two years of getting no action from the Senate, a coalition of citizens' organizations gathered a huge number of signatures to put a proposition on the ballot calling for the creation of a Coastal Commission. Proposition 20, as it was named, passed in the November elections by a margin of ten per cent. It set up a coastal commission with broad powers to limit coastal construction and preserve public access to beaches. The Commission was empowered to require coastal cities and counties to submit Local Coastal Programs regulating development and protecting public interest. Where the local governments failed to do so the Commission could intervene to enforce action. One of its most significant sections is Article 3 which covers recreation, placing a priority on public and private recreation over residential development.

However Proposition 20 was a stop-gap measure which required passage of enabling legislation within four years and here the vested interests might once more have intervened to frustrate the wishes of the environmentalists. The very conservative California Governor, former film star Ronald Reagan who went on to become the nation's president, was nearing the end of his second term and he might have intervened to block or water down the provisions of Proposition 20. But in 1974 Democrat Jerry Brown, son of a former governor Pat Brown, was voted into office. The younger Brown seemed a product of the flower power and hippie movement then sweeping California. He was given the name of "Governor Moonbeam" and the goals of Proposition 20 were very much up his street. In 1976 he signed into law the California Coastal Act which set up the California Coastal Commission as a permanent government agency.

On the very likeable Ronald Reagan, I like to recall one of my favorite stories about him which concerned his intervening to protect public beach access. Malibu's only large stretch of public sand, Zuma Beach, is for its upper third edged by beach villas and is more or less a private preserve. But it did have one or two footpaths allowing surfers to get through to the big waves. The occupant of one of the houses bordering a footpath decided to have done with the irritant of public passage and she fenced off the footpath and built a shuffle board on it. To her dismay she looked out a window and saw surfers toting huge boards hauling themselves over her fence, like a string of Amazonian ants carrying giant jungle leaves. They tramped over her shuffle board and headed for the waves. She called the local constabulary but they refused to intervene. A strong supporter and contributor to Republican causes, she decided to go right to the top, only to be told by the governor's office that the access footpath was public property and there was nothing the governor could do.

Due to the passage of the California Coastal Act, the environmental movement had by 1976 acquired all the legal powers it needed to protect the coastline. And by good luck it had also found the Man it needed to carry out its wishes.

Peter Douglas, born Peter Ehlers in Berlin, arrived in the United States in 1950 after a sea voyage which, as he later disclosed, had imbued him with a profound love of the oceans. He changed his surname after acquiring United States citizenship. Opting for a career in law, he began working as a legal assistant to a State assemblyman in the early 70's. This was a time when demands for coastal protection were at a peak and Douglas was handed the job of drafting coastal legislation. This initial assignment set him on the road to becoming a key figure in the drawing up of environmental initiatives. He was the principal author of Proposition 20 and helped write the Coastal Act of 1976. After serving as the commission's chief deputy, he became executive director in 1985, a post he held until his retirement in 2011 due to ill health.

This post of executive director gave him immense powers and Douglas was determined to use them. His recommendations to the 12-member commission were rarely overruled and these recommendations revealed that he was a determined battler. Steve Blank, a long serving member of the Commission, described him as "the world's best bureaucratic street fighter."

Among other adversaries, he took on the heirs of legendary Californian publisher William Randolph Hearst whose life was fictionalized by Orson Welles in the classic movie "Citizen Kane." The Hearst family, which owned the publisher's castle San Simeon and vast acres of the central Californian coastline around it, wanted to build a resort and golf course. Douglas recommended that the commission reject the proposal on the grounds it would have restricted beach access and intruded on sensitive wildlife habitats and the commission followed his recommendation.

During his tenure the agency secured 1,300 easements for paths to the shore through private property. It helped create thousands of acres of parkland and coastal trails. He was not averse to taking on the most powerful figures of Hollywood, who, liberal though they might be in their national politics, turned profoundly conservative when fighting the intruding barbarians who left scraps of paper or an occasional tin can on the beaches fronting their houses. Hollywood mogul David Geffen fought for years to block public access to the small strip of beach in front of his Malibu mansion before giving in under Commission pressure and accepting a compromise which allowed public access but placed a number of limitations on it.

What Douglas achieved was a miracle as Coastal Commissioner Steve Blank acknowledged in an interview with the *Los Angeles Times*. All you had to do, he said, was drive from San Francisco to Los Angeles down what is today one of the world's great uncluttered nature strips and ask yourself "How the heck did we do this?"

"It doesn't take bad planning or bad decisions to have a billboard or hotel every 100 yards. Instead it takes a consistent view of what the Coastal Act says." And this, Blank said, is what Peter Douglas provided.

But in enforcing the conditions of the Coastal Act, Blank added, "Peter brought down the wrath of everybody who believed otherwise."

Peter Beard, an official of the developer-oriented Pacific Legal Foundation, charged: "Under Douglas's leadership, the Commission became the rogue agency that it is, running roughshod over people's rights, destroying economic opportunity and, ironically, make it unaffordable for all but the wealthiest to buy land in California's coastal zone."

Douglas himself said he had survived eleven attempts to have him fired from the Commission. From its inception, Commission opponents sought to weaken it by cutting its budget and to a considerable degree they succeeded. The Supreme Court, highest judicial body in the land, stripped it of some of its enforcement powers by denying it the right to compel land owners to provide public access and saying the commission had to buy the land for such access like every private business operation.

The Coastal Commission is supposed to review Local Coastal Programs every five years but its skimpy budget makes this impossible for it to do this.

Nevertheless one Coastal Program had become a pressing matter. Los Angeles County was chafing at the restrictions put on it by its initial Marina del Rey Coastal Program and it was pressing for a review. It wanted changes in residential densities and the right to build on protected parking lots which it regarded as under utilized.

In May 1995, a general debate took place on the future of Marina del Rey which revealed a split among the 12 Coastal Commissioners. Two of the commissioners said they felt the local authority, Los Angeles County, should be left to decide on Marina development and that the County could be relied on to act within the terms of the California Coastal Act.

Others felt strongly that the Commission's job was to uphold the Coastal Act and not leave it to the County. They felt it was incumbent on the Commission to strike a balance between recreational uses and the County's need for revenue to maintain Marina facilities.

Commissioner Gary Giacomini, who emphasized this need for balance, said: "I believe that if you went whole hog for the County and gave them everything they wanted, well, you can just forget all about it is going to provide a significant public recreational facility, because all it is going to be is just yet again, another set of development that is so sad when you go up and down this coast, and it walls off the use of the public on the coast, which is what we exist to protect."

Alternate Commissioner J. Hisserich said: "I think it is safe to say that as one who goes to the Marina on a regular basis... there is inadequate recreation opportunities and far too much development."

As there was a divergence of opinion, the Commissioners opted to leave it to Commission staff to iron out differences with the County and come to a final agreement on the new Marina Local Coastal Program.

Before the amended Marina Local Coastal Program was finally approved in 1996, the Commission made several major concessions. It agreed to the County authorizing an additional 1,000 residential units on the Marina's west side in exchange for the County designating a two-acre lot known as Parcel FF for a public park. The County agreed to billing developers $600 for every new residential unit before issuing them their building permits. This money was to be paid into a Coastal Improvement Fund to be used for projects like the FF park.

The Commission also wanted 15.5 acres reserved as open space on the west side to compensate for overbuilding of residential blocks but it finally went along with a County proposal to reserve 12.7 acres. As this included more than ten acres of a flood retention basin, most of which was either underwater or exposed mud, Commission staff admitted the public was getting a particularly poor deal.

Commission staff raised an issue over the Abe Lurie abandoned hotel project which was then a fenced off weedy expanse. The County applied to turn this into another apartment block but staff said it could not consider making this a low-priority residential unit in place of a visitor-serving hotel and it recommended turning it into a park. Faced with the possible loss of control over a valuable waterside site, the County rushed in to say it had changed its mind and wanted to retain the site as a hotel. To sweeten the deal it proposed to drop plans for converting a nearby parking lot, labelled OT, into an apartment block.

Deputy Commission director Chuck Damm made it clear that on one issue the Commission had no intention of yielding, that was permitting building on the Marina's 13 parking lots which were protected as either parks or parking. "Staff recommendation would not allow for the public parking lots to be converted to private use, primarily residential use," he said. "Staff believes that the Marina already has a very strong residential component, in fact too much residential."

Commission Executive Director Peter Douglas, in the brief contribution he made to the debate, said: "This Commission, as have others, have consistently taken the position that (the) bond measure, which was approved by voters to create a public recreational facility, that the development of that facility has not, in our opinion, met those promises… That is why we feel so strongly about the recommendation relative to park uses. Residential uses are not consistent with that policy, and that promise."

With the limited concessions agreed to by the County including the promise to build a park on FF, Douglas determined that the amendments to the Coastal Program were legally adequate and it was certified by the Commission and enacted by the County into law.

CHAPTER EIGHT

"Forget it, Jake"

In 2000 I became a resident of Marina del Rey.

My wife and I were living in Paris but we came to Los Angeles for two reasons: the wedding of the daughter of a close friend and urgent cancer surgery for me. And having landed there, we stayed. We took up residence in a tower apartment complex known as Marina City Club. From our balcony six floors up we enjoyed a spectacular view of the waters of the Marina and the comings and goings of sailboats, speedboats and rowing boats.

During the following two or three years I became deeply attached to the Marina, not just for the beauty of Mother's Beach but also for the encounters with marine life we experienced on our daily walks — fish churning the waters and leaping up into the air, seals coming far up into the Marina in pursuit of the fish and filling the silence of the night waters with their barking, and — most beautiful of all — the great blue herons standing statue-like on the prows of boats, their eyes rigidly fixed on the waters below for any signs of fish. Added to the great blue herons, the night herons, the pelicans, the terns, the martins, and an occasional osprey.

It took a while before my affection for the Marina sparked my curiosity about Marina politics. A number of organizations were militating at that time for the preservation of recreation and public parking. I was eventually drawn to a little group called WeAREMarinadelRey. The co-directors of this organization were a good-looking businesswoman and recreational sailor Nancy Marino and David Barish, a dedicated backpacker who had migrated from New York to Los Angeles where he ran his backpacker business alongside working for Marina preservation. Nancy at times would get stressed under the pressures of her business responsibilities and Marina activism but when she took the stand at the various public hearings and began with "Good evening, honorable commissioners — or whatever they were — my name is Nancy Vernon Marino" her arguments came across as clear as a bell. Then there was Dan Gottlieb, a retired mathematics professor, who could be relied on for studying the fine print and nitty gritty of official documents, and Lynne Shapiro, a former schoolteacher, who could dash off a letter to editors of local newspapers at the drop of a hat. And the most extraordinary of all, Carla Andrus, who had moved from a rather unpleasant south central Los Angeles existence with its attendant violence, to the Marina where she lived on a small boat. Carla's little boat covered by tenting to protect it from the rain, was a floating archive of Marina documents. She turned up to meetings of our group with at least two supermarket plastic shopping bags full of the documents we needed for that day's deliberations. Carla was the activist equivalent of the pitbull, never letting up in her fierce dedication to preserving public rights and exposing administrative boondoggles in the Marina.

At the urging of that assembled cast I occasionally attended meetings of the Marina Design Control Board, the Smallcraft Harbor Commission, the County Regional Planning Commission, the Los Angeles Board of Supervisors, Environmental Impact debates and other public hearings on Marina planning. But I became more deeply involved when an announcement from the County Beaches and Harbors Department about planned development of the Marina known as Phase II had the shattering effect on me of a bombshell.

That department announced it intended shutting down the picnic area of Mother's Beach and the safe sandy launch pad for non-powered boats like outriggers and kiddies' rubber dinghies, and moving both over to the inland side of the Marina where there was no sand. I found this announcement simply stupefying but I was also surprised by the lack of attention it got in the local press. The major newspapers of Los Angeles County ignored it.

At this point Carla and I put our heads together. The lack of newspaper coverage meant that the 10 million residents of Los Angeles County had not been informed about what was afoot and there was little hope of a widespread citizens' reaction. The County was probably counting on that to make sure its proposal went through.

I figured that although Los Angeles residents as a whole might not know much about the County's plans there was one lot of residents who weren't going to like Phase II one bit. They were the families who drove from all over the county on weekends and holidays to have their picnics on the tables of Mother's Beach. Carla's eyes lit up at my suggestion that we could forge a protest movement from the ranks of the picnickers. "Great idea," she said. I went off to a local printery to get hundreds of cards printed up. In the end we needed hundreds more. The picnickers took to the protest campaign with enormous enthusiasm. Carla had a set speech telling them that the County proposed shutting down the picnic area alongside the sand where their children played and shoving them over to an inland area of the Marina where there was no sand. When she was finished the picnickers rushed to grab the cards out of our hands. They interrupted lunches and games to hand around pens and get every person at their table to sign. Some told us that they had been coming to Mother's Beach each summer since childhood and they couldn't imagine the Marina without the picnic tables. Some asked for extra cards to take home to their friends and during the course of the succeeding week these cards were posted back to us.

On Saturdays and again on Sundays Carla and I turned up with our cards. And on Monday we posted them off to the California Coastal Commission office in Long Beach. It took a while before we got a reaction from official-dom but when it came it was exactly what we wanted to hear. Peter Douglas confided in David Barish, co-director of WeAREMarinadelRey, that there was one part of the County's plan that was off the table. "IR?" David asked. That was the Mother's Beach picnic area and parking lot official designation. Douglas nodded.

I wouldn't wish to claim that it was our protest card campaign that was responsible for this decision. But the least one can say is that flood of cards delivered to the commission offices early each week can't have hurt.

Carla and I had got what we wanted and the picnickers had got to keep their barbecue grills on Mother's Beach. Perhaps it was time to wind up my involvement in Marina politics. Running from one hearing to another on the Phase II permitting process, was becoming more time consuming and boring. The County's actions were growing more and more devious and it was pretty clear they were taking no notice of the little speeches we made expressing our opposition.

Perhaps at that point I should have heeded the advice offered to Jake Gittes (Jack Nicholson) when he proposed to press on with his investigation of official malfeasance at the climax of the Roman Polanski film.

"Forget it, Jake," his colleague told him. "It's Chinatown."

CHAPTER NINE

The Mermaids

However I found it wasn't so easy to forget.

Perhaps civic activism is a form of addiction. Although I doubt that, as many who joined our ranks of Marina preservers were as prone to leave as they were to join.

Perhaps the Sunday morning meeting of our group had become an ingrained habit. We met regularly at 10 o'clock every Sunday at the little dockside café The Mermaids and it was a pleasant addition to the routine that there was a cause to go along with the steaming cup of coffee.

Most of the group were experts in the intricacies of state and municipal regulation. Some had computer expertise at their fingertips. They prepared the slide shows which were given at committee meetings.

My job was to write up and distribute press reports to get public attention to what was going on in the Marina. And in my books there was plenty that needed attention. Beside the shutting down of the Mother's Beach picnic tables, the County was also planning to give away the boatyards on the east side of the Marina for shopping malls and cram the boats into an unsightly boat stacking tower dominating the natural landscape of the Ballona wetlands, handing over the lots promised for a public park and parking in 1996 for more apartments, grabbing at least three parking lots supposed to be preserved for either parks or parking for more private developments, and the construction of a waterside office tower to house the officials of the Beaches and Harbors Department themselves. In the Phase II plans there was not a single word about recreation apart from a proposed expansion of a park on the eastern side of the Marina where the department planned to dump the picnickers it kicked out of Mother's Beach. As far as recreation was concerned, Phase II was a great big Minus.

Among the members of our little group with their assigned tasks, I must honestly rank myself the least successful. Nothing seemed to dent the general press indifference to what was going on in the Marina. My pleas to the *Los Angeles Times* to turn an investigative eye on what the County was proposing to do in Phase II got nowhere. My press releases resulted in an occasional visit of a television crew or a local newspaper reporter looking for a color story but that was all. I think this lack of press coverage spilled over into an erosion of local support for our campaign. Gradually our members drifted away, perhaps under the toll of other commitments or the fact that our campaign to get the County to change tack seemed to be getting nowhere, and in the end we were reduced to a hard core of dedicated campaigners, determined to stay in the battle to the end.

A footnote to the story of our little protest group. Eventually the Mermaids cafe vanished, itself a victim of the County's grandiose re-development plans. It was torn down to make way for a private 5-story parking garage.

CHAPTER TEN

The Vanishing Media

I got the job of press agent for WeAREMdR at a time of profound change in the Los Angeles media scene. During the first thirty years or so the local media had kept County actions in the Marina squarely under its sights. This applied particularly to the *Los Angeles Times* which invested considerable editorial resources in its investigative reporting of Marina doings. But I arrived at a time when television and the Internet were cutting into the advertising revenues of the printed press. It was a time of staff cutbacks. The interest in Marina activities began to fade. This was to play an important role in what happened in the Marina over the next ten years.

A harbinger of this change was the disappearance of the daily *Santa Monica Outlook* in 1998. Santa Monica is the dominant city on Los Angeles County's westside and the decision of the *Outlook* owners to close the newspaper because of a drop-off in advertising left the city without a voice.

A journalist friend of mine, Ivor Davis, who worked for a time at the *Outlook*, describes it as a feisty newspaper which was locked in a constant battle with the much larger *Los Angeles Times* for scoops on developments in the western area of the city. Davis says the newspaper covered both County and Los Angeles city governments for any news affecting its readership.

Outlook owners cited loss of advertising as the main reason for shutting down but probably just as important in undermining their newspaper was the extraordinary rise to fame and fortune of the *Los Angeles Times*.

In the immediate postwar period the *Times* was a stuffy, right-wing rag which was only one of the newspapers on the Los Angeles scene. It had been in the hands of the Chandler family since 1882 and from the outset it had proclaimed itself stolidly pro-Republican. Among other causes it championed during its early years was the Owens Valley land grab to ensure an adequate water supply for the rapidly expanding city of Los Angeles.

In 1960 the paper's conservative stance was to change. The pro-Republican Norman Chandler handed over the role of publisher to his son Otis. The younger Chandler decided to challenge the dominance of east coast newspapers like the *New York Times* and *Washington Post* by turning the *Times* into a major national newspaper with highly competitive national coverage and Pulitzer prize-winning investigative reporting on local and national issues. As part of this move, he swung the *Times* into a centrist political position. I was flattered to be greeted by Chandler soon after my arrival in Los Angeles. He wished me luck in my enterprise of setting up a Reuter bureau in his city. A few years later the *Los Angeles Times* itself became a subscriber to the Reuter news service which was seeking to extend itself in the United States market.

In every way Chandler was Mr. Southern California. He was a golden-haired beach boy, a body builder of imposing muscular stature. Testimony to his impressive size was provided when he tried to enroll in an Air Force training program and was rejected because his frame would not fit into a jet. He was known to interrupt office business and rush off to the beach because he had got word that "surf was up." His editors hired some of the best writing talent in the country. It was exciting times to be working on that newspaper. Circulation soared into the stratosphere, topping 1,225,000 at its peak. The *Los Angeles Times* became a steamroller that flattened opposition. The *New York Times* tried to enter the California market but gave up (although it did return to the scene several years later). The inroads of the *Times* into the west Los Angeles area inevitably caused a drop off in *Santa Monica Outlook* circulation.

In the 1990's Los Angeles County was preparing to extend its privatization land grab in the Marina on two fronts — by renewing the leases of current developers for a further 39 years and to privatize other lots it had not yet given away. With the *Santa Monica Outlook* going through its death throes, the *Times* had the story largely to itself. And in the case of the lease extensions, the *Times* threw its whole weight into investigating the County's actions and criticizing the extensions as 'gifts' to favored developers.

But change was coming to the *Los Angeles Times* as well. In 1980 Otis Chandler gave up his role as publisher. Perhaps this essentially outdoors man had grown tired of the office grind. A friend said, "Otis has gone surfing and he's not coming back." However in 1999 he did come back. Appalled by the fact that the team that had taken over from him had fudged the lines between advertising and journalism he came out of retirement to blast the *Times* management in a letter addressed to the newspaper's staff. The *Times* had published a magazine about the new Staples center, home to its star basketball team, the Lakers, but had failed to tell its readers or reporters that it was sharing advertising revenue from the issue with the sports arena. Chandler called this "unbelievably stupid" and a "dangerous compromise to the newspaper's objectivity."

Probably because of his disgust over the Staples Center scandal, Chandler approved of the takeover of the *Times* by the Chicago-based Tribune Company in 2000, saying he thought the new management might shake the *Times* out of its torpor. He barely lived long enough — he died six years later — to learn that out-of-town ownership was not necessarily the answer.

Confronted with new forms of competition like television and the internet, *Times* circulation was now headed on a downward track. By 2006 it had fallen to 843,000, well below the million-plus of its glory days. Falling circulation and shrunken advertising revenue inevitably led to staff cuts and reductions in reporting resources. Bill Boyarsky who as City Editor from 1998 to 2001 steered *Times* editorial through the changeover from family ownership to the Tribune takeover, told me that Tribune management made a series of staggering cuts in editorial staff from 1,300 to about 500. A walk through the editorial floor reveals that a large number of reporters' booths, once bustling with reportorial activities, are now empty pods. Along with other departments, its West Los Angeles bureau covering key cities like Malibu, Santa Monica and Marina del Rey, was severely cut back. When the County embarked around the turn of the century on its second giveaway scheme in the Marina known as Phase II the *Times* fell strangely silent. The *Times* not only failed to report on the initial announcement on Phase II but it also omitted to cover any of the significant developments as the County pushed ahead with its giveaway plans. County officials can scarcely have believed their luck. The *Times*, by remaining silent, significantly facilitated their schemes.

It is not hard to explain how this incredible lapse in Times coverage came about. The Western bureau of the *Times*, depleted by staff reductions, failed to get on to the story from the very outset. And having failed to put its foot on the pedal from the start it quickly became outpaced by the sequence of events, the progression of the story from one permitting meeting to another. The only newspaper which took on this responsibility was a weekly called *The Argonaut*, founded by publisher David Asper Johnson to cover the development of the Marina. The story of the County's mismanagement of the Marina can be found chronicled in its pages. Much of that chronicling was done by my good friend Helga Gendell who contributed a lot of the information to the earlier chapters of this book.

By hammering away at *Times* editorial I did manage to get a couple of reporters down to speak with us. But the stories they wrote portrayed us as Marina residents who were out to preserve the comforts of our ocean side lifestyle. This was 180 degrees from the truth. Our small group, far from being NIMBYs (acronym for Not In My Backyard), was putting all its efforts into ensuring the ten million residents of Los Angeles County would have recreational facilities and parking access to the waters of the Marina. The couple of stories which made it into the *Times* pages gave the County a further opportunity to trumpet the fact that all they were doing was upgrading the out-of-date Marina and I don't think my colleagues felt these stories did much to help our cause.

CHAPTER ELEVEN

The Slipping Slips

The principal leisure attraction of Marina del Rey is, of course, boating.

The Marina was created in the immediate postwar years as a small-craft harbor to provide about 6,212 slips for recreational boating, defined at that time as slips of less than 35 feet. In those less opulent times more than 80 per cent of recreational boats were said to be of that size while less than one per cent were of the luxury yacht category of 100 feet or more.

But Wall Street and the California housing boom changed all that. Larger yachts, symbols of status, appeared on the scene, touching off an ongoing debate as to whether so many of the smaller slips were needed. The debate played into the hands of Marina developers and County officials who were intent on creating more profitable larger slips to go along with their luxury apartments. Claims were made constantly that there was a very high vacancy rate in the smaller slips. The Department of Beaches and Harbors commissioned a boat slips survey which it said proved that point. But department critics claimed the figures had been cooked by listing a large number of small slips as 'vacancies' which, in fact, were part of a building site which had been emptied of all boats and placed off limits to the public. The head of Beaches and Harbors publicly admitted as much during a 2009 hearing of the Small Craft Harbor Commission. Asked by a commissioner if these emptied slips might show up on statistics as 'vacancies', Beaches and Harbors director Santos Kreimann said: "I believe these vacancies would show up on our vacancy count." Commissioner Al Landini responded: "So its spurious. These are not true vacancies."

It is impossible for me as an outsider, and a non-boater at that, to sort through the conflicting figures and establish who is right in this argument. But as a constant walker round the Marina moles I cannot say that I ever saw a large amount of vacant slips.

In fact my impression was that the small-craft harbor concept of the Marina was an enormous success. On regatta days, trucks and motorcars from all over the state towing or cradling small boats converge on the Mother's Beach sandy launch pad and jam-pack the boaters' parking lot. But it is not necessary to wait for regatta days to gauge the success of the recreational boating Marina. On any weekend day, or even on some week days, the Marina main channel can be a breathtaking parade of swelling sails, sails of differing colors to represent yachting teams, white sails on student boats setting out from a university-run launch ramp with instructors in tenders yelling out commands over loud hailers, men's and women's rowing eights piercing through the confusion of yachts like swift arrows, bulky cruise ships looming above the busy traffic, paddle boarders and dinghies sticking to the safer, shallower edges of the channel, and, through it all, pelicans and terns dive-bombing from a great height and sending up spurts of water as they forage for fish.

Nevertheless, with the turn of the century, the constant demand by developers for bigger slips began to take a significant toll on the number of small affordable slips. The construction of high-priced rental apartments at the waters edge carried with it a demand by developers for the mooring of luxury yachts, something that was more in tune with their concept of the Marina for the well-to-do. The stage was set in the Phase II of Marina development when the Doug Ring organization absorbed a number of small boat docks into their gigantic Esprit One development. In the conversion of the docks they simply wiped out under 35 feet slips completely.

Jon Nahhas, of the Boating Coalition, a constant defender of the rights of small boat owners, has listed the steady erosion of the smaller slips since the year 2000. In 2001, the County and developers got together to establish that "a current situation existed" in which there was a low demand for affordable recreational boating. Nahhas says they asked the California Coastal Commission to allow the reduction of slips from 590 to 319, a net loss of 271 public slips. Nearly all the losses, he says, were in the under 35 foot category. Slips of 51 foot or greater had a net gain of 78.

In 2003 another developer who had his lease extended was back at the Coastal Commission demanding a slip reduction of 200. This time, Nahhas says, the Commissioners were considerably taken aback by this second request coming so soon after the reduction agreed to in year 2001. But a L.A. County official reassured them that there would be no more loss of the small slips.

But by the year 2011 the County had forgotten this promise, along with all the other promises it had made on preserving the recreational Marina, and with seven other lessees it came back to the Coastal commission asking for a massive reduction of 741 boat slips. Without any reference to the number of small slips that had already been removed and the County's prior promise to halt small slip removals, the Commission, on the recommendation of its staff, approved what was called the "Master Waterside Coastal Development Permit."

Once again some of the Commissioners tried to extract an undertaking from the County that no more slips would be lost but they were rebuffed by their own staff, deputy director Jack Ainsworth telling them that in the changing world of leisure boating imposing such arbitrary limits could prove impractical.

With this 2011 concession, the reduction of small slips had now reached truly spectacular levels. From the 6,000 slips created at the Marina's inception, most of them in the small slip category, the number of slips had fallen to 4,255, meaning more than one quarter of the original slips had been lost. But Nahhas says the elimination of small recreational boating slips is not to end there. A second Master Waterside Project involving six more privately-operated Marinas is in the works, he says, which will result in the elimination of 693 more small slips further decimating what he calls 'affordable boating opportunities'. This brings the total of small slips down to 3,562, most of them in the under 35 feet category. This is perilously close to half the original number and makes a mockery of the County's claim to be a suitable steward of the recreational Marina.

Nahhas says this steady erosion of smaller slips may eventually spell the doom of the recreational boating Marina. He says fewer boat slips will lead to higher fees and this will cause affordable boating to go away.

CHAPTER TWELVE

Spin, Lies and Videotape

Almost from the moment of getting the Marina Local Coastal Program certified by the Coastal Commission in 1996, Los Angeles County embarked on a campaign of breaking its promises and fabricating amendments and wordage to cover its subterfuges.

Very few lots remained in the Marina which were not already committed to private residential or commercial development. These included the protected parking lots and areas devoted to boating facilities. What Phase II set out to do was to change the designated use on many of these lots. Boat yards were to become shopping malls. Parking lots were to be turned into apartments, shops and offices.

But long before Phase II was announced the County had been working with existing lessees to extend leases which were supposed not to go beyond 60 years. The County also cooperated with the lessees to get Coastal Commission approval for tearing down some existing apartment blocks and rebuilding them to greater mass and heights.

The County's reason for all this reconstruction, as I have already said, was that the Marina was 30 years old and needed refurbishing. County Beaches and Harbors director Stan Wisniewski struck up the theme in a 1995 Coastal Commission meeting when he said of the Marina: "Unfortunately she is beginning to show her age." County Supervisor Don Knabe, the supervisor in charge of the Marina area, repeated it whenever he got a chance. As late as 2011 Knabe was quoted by the *Los Angeles Times* as saying the Marina was desperately in need of a tune-up. "It just needs to be polished," Knabe said.

No reporter seemed to want to take a closer look at that time to see how ridiculous all these statements were. If every building in Los Angeles which was 30 years old had to be torn down the City of Los Angeles would look like a hydrogen bomb hit it. Poorly constructed Marina docks which were the responsibility of the lessees might be rotting and tilting and in need of replacement but that was a much smaller matter. Apartment blocks might be crying for repairs but this was due to the lack of maintenance provided by the lessees who took advantage of the decay they themselves had instituted to make their case for getting extended and more ambitious leases. Friends of the Marina spokesman Ilene Weiss told the 1995 Coastal Commission meeting: "No enforcement. That's the real problem of the Marina. Lessees deferring maintenance for guaranteed lease expansions."

In the early nineteen-nineties the County offered the prospect of rich pickings to its favored developers by issuing an invitation for current leaseholders to apply for extensions. These offered extensions were themselves of dubious validity. The 1959 bond issue which paid for drainage, streets, sewers and other facilities had specified that leases issued to developers to help repay the bonds were not to extend beyond 60 years. The correct procedure would seem to have been to go back to the voters to get lease extensions approved. But the County appeared reluctant to do this perhaps because it was fending off a large amount of public criticism to its Marina management and feared the issue might not play as well with voters as it had in 1956. It simply concocted its own amendment with the advice of outside consultants and carried on with authorizing the lease extensions.

Jack Keating of the defunct *Los Angeles Herald-Express* had described the initial Marina leases as 'giveaway deals' in a 1961 series of articles. When it came to renewing the leases the *Los Angeles Times* led the charge.

The *Times* threw its editorial resources into studying a 39-year lease extension the County proposed to grant to one of the Marina's biggest leaseholders, Goldrich and Kest. It called on the opinions of real estate experts who found the proposed agreement badly wanting. A retired University of California professor Fred Case told the *Times* the deal would give the county far less than it should receive from the waterfront property.

"I don't think the County should touch it," he told reporter Jeffrey L. Rabin. "They should call in a consortium of people who usually handle lease investments and have them analyze it …. It ought to be recalculated."

Case said the County was "in effect selling the property" by extending the lease so far into the future. "Any lease arrangement over 50 years is in effect full ownership," he said.

Santa Monica real estate consultant Stephen Dietrich was even more blunt. He told the *Times*, "It's a gift."

Despite these warnings, the County Board of Supervisors went ahead and approved the deal which, it announced, would form the basis for future negotiations with other lessees.

The next to the trough was major Marina lessee Douglas Ring. A former aide to a County Supervisor and husband of influential city councilwoman Cindy Miscikowski, Ring had early on spotted the golden opportunity of

pushing himself forward as a Marina developer. The Ring operation was originally a three-way partnership between the Ring family, a second developer and
State Senator Alan Robbins, subsequently imprisoned. The second developer
died, and Ring, fearing that Robbins' imprisonment might jeopardize his business dealings, sued to limit Robbins' authority in the company, and he was left
in sole command.

The free newspaper *L. A. Weekly* took a close look at Ring's management
of his extensive Marina holdings in the course of these lease extension negotiations and was not impressed. *L.A. Weekly* reporter Lou Rutigliano wrote: "Ring
stands out as the one with the best political connections and the longest history
of political largess — he's been a major campaign contributor for decades — as
well as the Marina landlord with one of the worst records for maintenance and
tenant complaint," the newspaper said.

Rutigliano went on: "The deliberations over Ring's status raise questions
about the county's own performance. Based on the record to date, neither the
supervisors nor their minions at the Department of Beaches and Harbors have
proved capable of managing the competing interests and myriad problems aris-
ing from a public asset that some consider a crown jewel of L.A. County real
estate."

To a certain extent Ring and his associates had taken a calculated gamble
in snapping up a string of County leases early in Marina development. But
by 1998 the Marina was no longer a gamble. It was one of the hottest pieces of property on the Los Angeles County coastline. Ring claimed in a press
interview that his properties were overburdened with debt and to have any
chance of survival he needed the lease extensions. But once extension negotiations were underway, according to Rutigliano, he changed his tune and said his
Marina properties were now out of the financial woods and his earlier statement was no longer relevant. However the docks and apartments faced "serious
deficiencies" in maintenance, the property was deteriorated by "substantial deferred maintenance" and the only solution, Ring claimed, was to tear everything
down and start again (on a much bigger scale, of course).

Rutigliano said the state of the docks was due to Ring's failure to provide
adequate maintenance and he went on to list scores of deficiencies such as cracks,
dry rot and listing docks which had been investigated by Beaches and Harbors
inspectors. Beaches and Harbors officialdom leapt to the lessees' defence.
"Deferred maintenance is a serious problem," Beaches and Harbors director
Wisniewski told the *L.A. Weekly.* "And we've taken steps to deal with it."

My friend Carla Andrus became the intermediary between harassed tenants at another Marina property, the Neptune apartments, and the County.
The tenants were complaining of a long list of problems including water seep-

age through their ceilings on to their beds and defective plumbing but were getting no action from the lessee. Carla interviewed them and aired their complaints at a weekly meeting of the Board of Supervisors. But it was scarcely the office of the occupants of those Olympian heights to concern themselves with mortal problems like faulty plumbing. Supervisor Don Knabe appeared not to be paying much attention to what Carla was saying and when she finished he failed to respond. However Zeus, in the illustrious personage of Board chairman Mike Antonovich, deemed that some form of response was needed. Looking towards Knabe he said: "Don?" Knabe grumbled: "I'll ask Santos." (Santos Kreimann, the newly-appointed director of Beaches and Harbors.) And that was the end of that.

It seemed to be in the perverse nature of the County's dealings with its lessees, that the level of their offenses in properly maintaining their properties formed the yardstick for the amount of County largess they were accorded in the lease extensions.

Doug Ring was the offender I mentioned earlier who had not only failed to finish his building project within the contracted time but had failed to start it. While telling smaller contractors to get lost if they had failed to apply for lease extension within the legal time limit, the County agreed to give Ring an extension on his lease in exchange for a payment of one million dollars. In the supercharged Los Angeles real estate market of that time, one million dollars would scarcely have bought you the equivalent of a powder room in a beachside mansion. Yet this munificent dealing with Ring happened not once but twice. Four years later he still had not started work on his apartment project. The County accorded him another four years in exchange for a payment.

But the greatest prize was being reserved for the owners of the Neptune apartments with their host of disgruntled tenants. They were not only granted permission to rebuild their apartments to new heights but the County threw in the bonus of a contiguous block they had zoned in 1996 would be reserved for a promised public park — a considerable consolation prize.

Another applicant for lease extension and rebuilding, Del Rey Shores apartments, fell into a very different category. Here the tenants not only had no beefs with the lessee but they loved their apartments. Del Rey Shores was a series of low level garden-style apartment blocks separated by meandering walkways. It was a sea of tranquility in a world of bustle and speeding traffic. The neighbors of The Shores apartments sued the County over the height and residential density of the proposed new building and they were supported by Shores residents who were opposed to being thrown out of their apartments. Their lawyer was the ill-fated Richard Fine, condemned to perpetual solitary imprisonment for his handling of their case. If the County was sincere in its desire to preserve the luster of the Marina it surely would have wanted to keep Del Rey Shores the way it was. Particularly as the bulky, unsightly tower which eventually went up in its place scarcely enhanced the image of the neighborhood. Most of its neighbors are united in deploring its cumbersome, gaudy design.

CHAPTER THIRTEEN

When is a Park not a Park?

Somewhere in the years following the 1996 Coastal Commission certification of the amended Marina Local Coastal Program, the promised park suddenly wasn't a park anymore. The County surreptitiously changed the wording to make it a parking lot. Then the parking lot morphed once again into an "under utilized parking lot."

To our WeAREMarinadelRey Mathematics Prof, Dan Gottlieb, this was all part of the practice of officials surreptitiously changing words or inserting misleading or false clauses in a document. He says this form of official corruption has been given a number of names over the years — Coconut Roading, named for the beneficiary of a freeway connection earmark slipped illegally into an act of Congress, Waldo-ing meaning hiding a falsification in plain sight by burying it in a forest of complexity, (the name comes from a children's puzzle called 'Where's Waldo?'), malicious misprints, false addresses on building permit applications, outdated or incorrect maps, arbitrarily creating new parcel designations and finally just plain 'queering' or changing the meaning of words. Professor Gottlieb says Marina del Rey developments are liberally sprinkled with all of these.

In the mid 1990's when the County was currying favor with the Coastal Commission it had agreed to set up a Coastal Improvement Fund to pay for the promised park on parcel FF and other public amenities. The first developer stuck strictly by the rules. He agreed to provide paving and greenery around his apartment block in exchange for increased building height and other concessions and he paid a full contribution of $76,000 into the fund which was placed in an interest-bearing account. Proof of payment and the developer's agreement to other terms were passed on to the Executive Director of the California Coastal Commission who signed off on the deal and the building permit was issued.

Yet the County soon began playing the same games with the Coastal Improvement Fund as it was playing with the park itself. As new developments came on the scene, the County concessions went from barely comprehensible to downright frivolous. One builder was let off half his contribution to the Fund in exchange for re-paving a perfectly ordinary sidewalk around his building and adding various greenery touches – the sort of items that builders would be expected to pay for in any ordinary municipal housing contract. To add credibility to this concession the County redubbed the street around this building a "parkway."

The developers of another apartment complex, the Capri, didn't have to go to the lengths of claiming credits for a sidewalk in front of their building. They simply omitted the sidewalk completely. Pedestrians wanting access to the building's entrance have to walk out on the roadway – a situation which, it seems to me, must be fairly unique in apartment construction. This building was accorded the same height and density concessions as another across the road which had contributed fully to the development fund. But the Capri was let off contributing to the fund completely and the County says it is unable to produce any documentation to explain why.

Worse was to come. Up to this point the County had restricted itself to giving its dubious credits to amenities on the exterior of the buildings. It now went one step further and granted credits for amenities inside the complexes such as residents-only swimming pools and spas. A builder was let off entirely from contributing to the fund on the basis of credits granted for these amenities which were in the gated inner courtyard of his apartment complex. In other words a public fund was billed for providing private amenities in a luxury ocean side apartment block.

The mismanagement of the Coastal Improvement Fund was simply mind-boggling. The entire operation of the Fund disappeared into an administrative miasma. Payments which should have been made before a building permit was issued were made late and were not paid into an interest bearing account. The Coastal Commission appears not to have been informed of contributions to the fund. Part of this was simply due to administrative bungling. Management of the Fund was split between the County's Regional Planning Commission and the Department of Beaches and Harbors and one side seemed not to know about the moneys the other side was collecting and where they were being lodged. But the confused state of the Fund management also helped the County politically. It was able to put about that it was not possible to get started on building the promised park because there was not enough money in the fund to cover construction. Its low-balling of the amount of money in the fund was eventually to play an important role in the fate of the promised park.

The County was doing its full share of Coconut Roading or Waldoing or What You Will, but lessees were ever ready to get in on the act.

Builders Goldrich and Kest, lessees on a large parcel at the end of one of the Marina moles or fingers, applied to build an apartment block called Monte Carlo on their extensive land holdings. To win approval for increased building height and resident density they listed the project as congregate care senior housing. Congregate care facilities are designed for seniors who have been rendered less mobile by old age and they include such extras as having meals available. Goldrich and Kest said the meals would come from the adjacent Chart House restaurant, one of the pricier upscale restaurants in the Marina which would have made the occupants of Monte Carlo apartments among the most pampered seniors in recent Los Angeles history. This concession seemed improbable and indeed it was. Somewhere along the line the Monte Carlo morphed from a congregate care facility to a market rate for seniors 62 years old or older. The promised feast of gourmet cooking which had been so tantalizingly laid out before the old and infirm vanished with a puff. But Goldrich and Kest were not done with introducing their own little changes in the Monte Carlo. Opponents of the project discovered they were renting to people as young as 45 and the lessees were instructed to keep to their promise of renting only to age 62 and above. The congregate care classification requires far fewer parking lots for people who don't get around much any more. The lessees were given a parking variance which enabled them to provide a very limited quota of 30 parking spaces for the 60 units in the apartment block. In the automobile-oriented world of Los Angeles it goes without saying that one parking space for every two apartment units is wildly inadequate.

An even more tangled situation was developing on a project called Del Rey Shores which was closer to the ocean than the Monte Carlo and off the marina water's edge. This was the apartment whose neighbors sued against having their low-level (202) unit complex redeveloped into a five-story (544) unit block. Their suit eventually became entangled in the imbroglio over the jailing of lawyer Richard Fine and nothing came of it.

The rebuilding program at the Shores lay dormant for some years until a new Beaches and Harbors management, anxious to kick-start Marina construction in a period of financial recession, backed Shores developer Jerry Epstein's application to get a Federal Housing and Urban Development loan guarantee on the project. The loan guarantee was for $125 million dollars, the largest family units guarantee ever granted by HUD. WeAREMarinadelRey did not look favorably on the granting of such a huge loan backing for a high-density, luxury apartment complex which from the outset had been a target of controversy. Co-director David Barish submitted a Federal Freedom of Information request to HUD on March 2011 for background information on the granting of the loan guarantee and in mid-April he was sent a 125 page document containing all the facts.

Our Math Professor Dan Gottlieb lives in a neighboring apartment to the Shores and he was an opponent of the Shores redevelopment from the early Richard Fine days. His eagle eyes spotted something in the document which did not jibe with the facts. On page 5 of the Shores Mortgage Credit review needed to support the loan application he read: "Jerry Epstein (Trustee of Epstein Family Trust) — Jerry Epstein's credit history is very good as his credit scores ranged from 767 to 733, with no adverse findings. His HUD-92013-Supp also indicates no prior lawsuits or bankruptcies."

On May 2 Gottlieb shot off a letter to the HUD office of the Inspector General informing them that Epstein, as owner of Westside Condominiums LLC, underwent a bankruptcy which the judge did not discharge. "If the bankruptcies of Epstein LLCs are not counted in his HUD-92013-Supp, then HUD has a major flaw in its credit vetting process," Gottlieb wrote. "The fact that the Shores LLC and the Guaranty LLC have short credit histories should have raised the suspicions of the loan officers."

Gottlieb got no response to his missive but the reply that came to WeAREMarinadelRey was totally unexpected. In a letter from HUD attorney Edward J. Campbell, regarding the Shores loan documents, Barish was told: "We herein make demand that all of the above referenced documents and/or the information contained therein, and any copies thereof, within your and/or We ARE Marina del Rey's possession and/or control, be returned to HUD immediately… We also demand that any and all electronic copies of the above referenced documents and/or the information contained therein, and any copies thereof, within your and/or We ARE Marina del Rey's possession and/or control be destroyed immediately.

"Furthermore, given that these documents may contain private, sensitive, confidential and/or legally privileged information we demand that you immediately CEASE AND DESIST in making any and all disclosures of the aforementioned documents and/or the information contained therein. Additionally, any and all dissemination, including electronic disseminations, disclosure, distribution, use and/or copying of these documents and/or the information controlled therein is strictly prohibited." The HUD attorney demanded that the documents be returned to the HUD office within three business days.

Barish replied with a polite letter saying that he was willing to stop handing over the document to any third party but that HUD had to be aware that his organization had already loaned the document to an outsider and We Are Marina del Rey had no control over what this outsider might have done with it.

Within three days Barish got back a highly threatening letter saying that if he failed to return the documents and to name the organization which had been loaned the documents, he (Barish) and the outside organization might be sued by the submitter (the Epstein company, developer of The Shores complex).

The ongoing controversy was leaked in the press and a volunteer lawyer sprang to Barish's defense. On the basis of his advice Barish sent off a further letter, March 2011, saying:

"I understand that you believe that HUD made mistakes in its processing of my request. But I am not aware of any requirement in the Freedom of Information Act that a requester return records disclosed as a result of mistakes in the processing of a request." In other words, Tough cheese!

HUD replied once more saying that they were still investigating the matter but had essentially turned decision on any further action over to the Epstein organization.

And nothing further was heard about the legal threats.

Barish did make one minor concession. On the understanding that HUD would provide him with a revised response to his initial request he returned his copy of the document and got his $72.20 fee back.

Gottlieb's analysis of this subsequent HUD response was that it was completely worthless.

And he caught out the framers of the second response in a whopping Waldo.

"They altered the legal description of the property apparently in order to improve the confidentiality of the principals," he says.

CHAPTER FOURTEEN

"Get Creative, Stan"

The head of the County's Beaches and Harbors Department who initially pushed through the County's Phase II of Marina development was Stan Wisniewski, a long time employee of the County's beach operations. Wisniewski came across at permit meetings as a rather colorless but stubborn man who tended to bridle at any challenge to his decisions. He signed on with the County in 1967 as parking attendant at a west side beach parking lot and rose through the ranks to be named director of the Beaches and Harbors Department in 1983. To an outsider he appeared to be a controlling and suspicious boss. If he saw one of his staff chatting at a permit hearing with someone outside the department he would come up behind and growl: "Get back to your work." He was replaced as head of the department in 2008. A County obituary notice issued at the time of his motor-car accident death one year later he was described him as the key figure in formulating Phase II. "Stan was instrumental in overseeing the commencement of second-generation development in Marina del Rey," the statement says.

For Wisniewski, the first stop out of the starting gate for getting permits for the various Phase II projects was the Design Control Board, a five-member panel of urban developments and architectural experts appointed by the Board of Supervisors. This board was responsible for vetting all projects and either passing them along to the Regional Planning Commission or turning them down. The official gobbledegook for its responsibilities was providing an 'initial conceptual review'. The board was set up in the very early days of the Marina with broad powers over building design but with the Marina getting off to a slow start its powers were somewhat reduced in order to encourage developers and facilitate their permits. In the early 2000's, the board was chaired by Susan Cloke, an architect and recognized expert in design, landscape and urban planning. In general she stuck by her mandate of facilitating the passage of building projects. But there came a time when she found that the parking proposals of a number of projects around Mother's Beach were so loaded with inconsistencies that she recalled three projects for a second look. That was followed by another project which the board simply could not stomach. The County proposed to build a boat stacking tower looming over the nature panorama of the Ballona Wetlands. Cloke labelled the project 'a betrayal of public interest', a criticism which could scarcely be more damaging as the stacking tower was to be built on publicly-owned lands. Her fellow board members agreed with her and they threw the project out.

Cloke's actions and objections were clearly not playing well with Wisniewski. Seeing him get his back up at one of her criticisms, Cloke teased playfully: "Get creative, Stan".

But as it happened Wisniewski was not about to get creative. He was much more inclined to get even. The Board of Supervisors was leaned upon to gut the authority of the Marina Design Control Board. They voted to remove the board's authority to review new projects. In a slap in the face to Cloke and her fellow board members, they instructed the Board to limit itself in future to reviewing signage and color schemes, although this initial directive was eventually somewhat softened by allowing the board to make some belated contribution to conceptual design. Initial design approval was transferred to the County Department of Regional Planning. This body sat twelve miles away from the Marina in downtown Los Angeles. Originally it was put around that they would occasionally visit the Marina to study proposals and make their recommendations on the spot. I am not aware that they ever did.

Soon after, Susan Cloke resigned. In her resignation letter she said: "The Board of Supervisors' action delegates the responsibility to review site planning, building footprint and building massing in Marina projects to the Regional Planning Commission. To my mind, this was a mistake for three reasons. One, Regional Planning is based downtown and cannot reasonably be expected to hold monthly evening meetings in the Marina, so location and scheduling will be obstacles to full public participation. Two, site planning is a basic component of urban design and removing that asks the board to do the work without all the tools. Three, it doesn't make common sense to appoint architects, landscape architects, urban designers, engineers and local business people to a board and then not fully use their abilities, the very reasons they were appointed."

In her resignation letter she said: "The Board of Supervisors motion redefining the responsibilities of the Design Control Board will, I think, make it more difficult for the county to protect the Marina environment and to plan for the successful future of the Marina."

At the same time as the Design Control Board was experiencing problems, Wisniewski was running into headwinds of his own. His boss, Supervisor Don Knabe, in a speech made in the Marina in 2005, recognized that the shutting down of the Mother's Beach picnic tables to make way for a twin-towers hotel project was controversial. He later expressed reservations about Wisniewski's proposal for building a Beaches and Harbors office building in the heart of the Marina.

The person who replaced Wisniewski when he was retired in 2008 was his assistant Santos Kreimann, a much more flexible operator with strong political sensitivities. Unfortunately these administrative talents were put to pushing through most of the giveaways of public land that Wisniewski had not survived to see through. He started well. His first very welcome action was to make arrangements for taking the controversial Mother's Beach picnic grounds handover off the board. With possible encouragement from Santos, the developer voluntarily withdrew its hotel project on the picnic and parking area.

In the wake of the Coastal Commission revealing that the Mother's Beach development had been cancelled, Carla and I lamented the fact that our protest drive had not extended to the kayakers, rowers, paddle-boarders and other non-powered boaters on the northern side of Mother's Beach. The continued use of their sandy launch-pad, particularly for regattas which drew boaters from all over the state, was threatened by the takeover of their parking lot across the road from the beach. A developer proposed to build an apartment/commercial structure on that lot. To appease the strong criticisms of the boaters, he offered to reserve 69 parking spaces in his underground parking for the exclusive use of the boaters. This was just one of the silly proposals that kept cropping up in Phase II. To begin with, 69 parking spaces were entirely inadequate for regatta events. On those occasions the existing parking lot was completely full. Added to that, the mere thought of rowers struggling out of an underground parking garage with their long and unwieldy rowing Eights was totally ridiculous.

As it happened, the non-powered boaters, led by the outrigger users, were well equipped to take care of themselves. Kreimann originally supported the building project on their parking lot, but a Board of Supervisors meeting at which the non-powered boater confraternity turned out in force to protest the loss of parking may have persuaded him to side with the boaters. At that meeting, lawyer Barry Fisher accused the County of proposing to move the users of small boats, including kiddies with their rubber dinghies from the sandy and safe launch on Mother's Beach, to a deep water launch on the other side of the Marina which he said was unsafe. Kreimann subsequently moved to eliminate the boaters' parking lot project from Phase II. This decision, although welcome news, had the result of splitting the opposition to Phase II at a critical juncture. The boaters, counting on their favored relationship with Kreimann, no longer had any need for working with WeAREMarinadelRey.

Needless to say the County was highly satisfied with Kreimann's effective handling of his Beaches and Harbors assignment. He became the go-to man for dealing with major County problems and was eventually elevated to a top post in the County administrative hierarchy.

CHAPTER FIFTEEN

The Pipeline

Early in my activist days I asked Nancy Marino, co-director of WeARE-Marina del Rey to explain to me what the County was up to in the Marina.

"They're going to run us all ragged by piecemealing the project and making us run from one meeting to another," she said. "And then they're going to put all the pieces together and ram it through the Coastal Commission."

The piecemealing went on unrelentingly between 2006 and 2009. Except County officials protested that they weren't piecemealing. If there is another word for what they were doing I am not aware of it. To take an example the County hired an urban planning firm to draw up a plan for developing Mother's Beach. The firm came up with all sorts of exciting ideas for non-powered boating activities on the northern end of the beach. Yet when I drew the attention of the head of the urban planning team to the fact that the County planned to put apartments on the parking lot over the road which would make her projects impractical, she said their brief did not extend to that side of the road.

WeAREMarina del Rey and others pleaded with the County to come up with a Master Plan which would permit discussion on a sensible mix of public recreation and access and private projects, County officials shot back, with a degree of sophistry that had become common to all of their statements, that what they were proposing WAS a Master Plan.

The County's main consultant on Marina development was a highly efficient operator called Andi Culbertson. Her job was to keep the County out of the sort of troubles that had marred the first phase of Marina development and she did a remarkably effective job. Culbertson sat in on some of the Marina planning meetings. At public hearings she was a discreet figure sitting towards the back of meeting rooms keeping a watchful eye on the County's interests.

After four years of the permitting process on various Phase II projects the time was approaching for what Nancy Marino had predicted would be a major change in County tactics — merging all the projects into a single proposal to put before the California Coastal Commission.

This came about through a process known as the "Road Map Approach."

Coastal Commission rules allow for only three amendments per year for each Local Coastal Plan revision. If the County had been restricted to three wishes like the characters in fairy stories, it would have been in very serious trouble indeed. It wanted to push through a whole bunch of amendments to give it almost total control over Marina development. Top of its wish lists were building permits it had pledged to various lessees which still needed retroactive Coastal Commission approval. But beyond that it had a host of other issues like getting control over the parking lots and changing permitted land use on vast stretches of boating yards. The answer to its problems was to bundle all these requests into one monster amendment which was given the name of the Road Map. At the time the Road Map issue came up the suggestion was put around that it was the idea of Commission Executive Director Peter Douglas. I found this hard to believe. Why should the hero of California's coastal protection propose a plan which would do tremendous harm to the recreational Marina? But some of my colleagues in WeAREMarinaDelRey were more inclined to believe it. As early as the 1996 amendment they had faulted Douglas for compromising with the County rather than upholding the terms of the California Coastal Act.

The County's push to hand over large areas of the Marina to private interests was now gathering momentum. They picked out six projects from the overall Roadmap Plan which would require Coastal Commission approval and cobbled these together in what they called the Pipeline Project. The so-called Pipeline included the picnic area and parking lot of Mother's Beach which was still on the Phase II books despite the hotel developer withdrawing his proposal, the non-powered boaters' parking lot, the promised park, a seniors' home on a promised parking lot, the conversion of considerable area of yacht and powerboat facilities into a shopping mall and other commercial uses and the construction of the boat stacking tower which the Design Control Board had thrown out calling it a 'betrayal of public interest', but which the County had simply reinstated at a higher level.

When the Pipeline Project came before the Board of Supervisors, we managed to stir enough interest within the Marina to fill a bus going downtown to the Supervisors' meeting. Some of the riders came with prepared speeches opposing the pipeline and others went along for the ride and to fill out the numbers. At one point in the bus ride a stylish felt hat I had acquired in an extended stay in Rome was lifted from my head and passed among the passengers to gather contributions. We managed to collect enough money to pay for renting the bus and give the driver a hefty tip.

David Barish was the principal speaker presenting the opposition to the Pipeline. At the beginning of his speech he called on all those supporting him to stand up and the bus passengers behind him rose to their feet. But if

Barish could exhibit a sizeable amount of support, the backers of the Pipeline, for the most part Marina lessees and dock managers, also turned out a large following.

The Supervisors voted for the Pipeline Projects but it was not the final vote on the matter. This took place at a later Board meeting which was much less well attended because by this time most people regarded County approval as a foregone conclusion. Nevertheless Dan Gottlieb and I opted to go downtown on an early morning bus to sit in on this final stage.

I made a speech which the Supervisors seemed to listen to intently, pleading with them to keep to their promises to build the promised FF park in the west side of the Marina and retain another lot for parking as promised in 1996. I wound up my speech by saying that the Marina belonged to the ten million inhabitants of the County and not to the few thousand apartment residents the County planned to shove in there. I have never thought of myself as much of an orator but this time, it seems, I rose to the occasion. People behind me in the large auditorium who were there to speak on entirely different issues broke into applause.

But my satisfaction on discovering my oratorical talents was short lived. Something much more important was happening in the rows of seats behind. County consultant Andi Culbertson was occupying her usual discreet position towards the back of the hall. I saw her nudge a man sitting behind her who strode forward to the podium microphone and told the Supervisors that discussions on Phase II developments had been going on for years and it was now time to put the matter to a final vote.

The Supervisors voted for the Pipeline and that, as far as County procedures were concerned, was the end of the matter.

Now it was onward to the California Coastal Commission.

CHAPTER SIXTEEN

"In the blink of an eye"

The days of Peter Douglas's spirited defense of the California coastline were coming to a close and doubts were being expressed as to whether the California Coastal Commission would have much clout after he was gone.

One of the long-standing commissioners and a close friend of Douglas, Steve Blank, made a very gloomy prediction. "Once he's gone, this commission will implode in the blink of an eye," Blank said. "And all we'll be talking about is the color of the concrete used to pave over what's left of the coast."

There was one member of the Commission who had a similar taste for battle as Douglas in defending the public's rights to coastline access. That was Sara Wan, of Malibu, California State Senate appointee on the commission from 1996, its longest serving member and chairman for two terms.

A native New Yorker and a graduate in biology and zoology, she told me how she had become an environmentalist on a journey across the United States. Her husband Larry had been given the job in 1962 of founding a school of engineering at the University of California Santa Barbara and they travelled across the northern states camping out in National Parks. "Seeing the magnificence of the west, I thought, 'My God we have to protect this,'" she said. "By the time I got to California, I was an environmentalist."

They moved to Malibu in 1985 and became involved in that coastal area's successful fight for cityhood.

As a coastal activist Wan was not averse to putting herself between property owners upholding California's wacko mean high tide line of public beach access and citizens who were being harassed while walking along the beaches. Learning from a newspaper article of someone who had gone to a local beach and been chased off by armed guards, she decided to check out the situation for herself. Taking her husband, the newspaper reporter and a newspaper photographer with her, she took up position on a part of the beach she knew from her research was a public easement. She didn't have to wait long before a beach guard confronted her little party. When she refused to move, the guard called the sheriff's office and no fewer than five police rolled up in all-terrain vehicles.

A female officer asked her if she had read the notices posted along the beach and Sara went over and read one which said the mean high tide line was a further 40 feet out to sea. "That put it right out in the ocean," she told me. When the officer had given her a lecture about trespassing Sara said, "Are you finished? Now let me tell you what the law is. In the first place the mean high tide line has to be determined by the California Lands Commission and not by property owners. And secondly the public has a right to be on this place where I'm standing." Sara told me, "I was well prepared and they were not."

It was somewhat unusual for a Malibu resident to become involved in Coastal Commission policies. Environmental preservation was not a top priority with the newly formed Malibu City Council and public access to the beach certainly was not. Malibu authorities, having freed themselves from being ruled directly by the Los Angeles County Board of Supervisors, did not welcome finding themselves beholden to the rules of the Coastal Commission, particularly on having areas of their city designated as environmentally sensitive habitat because that would have limited development. That meant that after she was made a Coastal Commissioner in 1996, she was often criticized as betraying the interests of her own city.

Asked what she felt were her main contributions to coastal preservation, Sara put her fight against the planting of non-native invasive species at the top of the list. "They take over the habitat and destroy it for the native species so that's a major, major contribution to the loss of species," she said. Among her other successes she lists the setting up of a task force to tackle the issue of contaminated sediments in the ports of Long Beach and Los Angeles and the introduction of water quality checks.

She was ever-ready to challenge the studies of self-styled experts she thought were ridiculous, and this applied particularly to presenters of traffic studies claiming proposed developments would not affect traffic. A victim of traffic jams in and around the Marina herself, she shot back at a traffic expert presenting soothing figures to say there was no traffic problem in the Marina. "Are you going to the same Marina as I go to?"

On the reduction of smaller recreational boat slips granted during her time on the Commission, she says: "I found that personally offensive. The Coastal Act specifically encourages low cost recreation. Now boating of any sort is not low cost but to push out individual boating slips in favor these big boats for the wealthy people goes against the spirit of the Coastal Act. It is inconsistent with the Coastal Act and I find it objectionable."

But the biggest surprise of my interview with Sara was on the question of the Road Map proposal. I told her it was being put around that this was Peter Douglas's idea. "This came up during my time," she says. "And it WAS Peter

Douglas's idea. Peter did many wonderful things for the California Coast but when he thought an issue was not important enough and opposing it might stir problems in Sacramento (California State capital) which would harm the Commission, he would knuckle under. It was a way of letting the County do what it wanted to do. I was opposed to it. ... The County got what it wanted. One of the big things to remember is that this is land that was purchased with public funds for the purpose of public recreation. OK? And it has been converted so that its primary function is generation of income for the County of Los Angeles — and I don't even know how much income it generates — but presumably that's why they do it, and then they give it away."

As I was visiting in the San Francisco region soon after her reappointment as Commission chair I thought I would take the opportunity of informing her and the other commissioners that one of the most important issues in Commission history was about to be brought before them. This, I said, was the question of citizen's rights to recreation and public access on the publicly-owned lands of Marina del Rey. I was gratified to see that Mrs. Wan was giving me her fullest attention.

What I could not know was that the Commission sitting at the tables in front of me was "toast," as the saying goes. By the time that the amendment of the Marina del Rey Local Coastal Program came before the Commission, six of the commissioners and the chairperson herself would be gone.

CHAPTER SEVENTEEN

The Commissioners

In the fifteen years between the 1996 amendment and Oceanside, the County worked tirelessly to gain complete control over the lands of the Marina free of any sort of oversight. They eliminated any form of independent review by gutting the powers of their Design Control Board. They kept their plans below the media radar by relentless piece-mealing. They refused to grant requests for a Master Plan which would have led to entertaining other ideas for the development of the Marina beside their own. They barreled ahead with granting permits and allowing extended leases even where these actions would require retroactive Coastal Commission approval. They surreptitiously changed terms for promised projects ('under utilized parking lot' for 'undeveloped park', for instance.)

But what they were doing went far beyond switching terms and 'queering' the meaning of words. To push their plans through they hired handsomely-paid consultants. These were not consultants as a member of the public might understand the term. They were not paid just to present a report containing ideas on which the County administration could act. They were hired to do the grunt work of pushing their ideas through to fruition, and thus became an extension of County administration itself. This put Marina developments one further step beyond the public purview.

There were three examples in which consultants played major roles. The first was giving the County a way of escaping from the condition in the original bond issue which said leases were not to extend beyond sixty years. As a result of their advice, the County passed an amendment and proceeded to grant lessees an extension for 39 years. The other two examples were consultants designing and pushing through what was eventually named the Road Map and pushing for a further major reduction in small boating slips in 2011.

In effect, the County was spending taxpayers' money to finagle the public out of their ownership of publicly-owned land.

When it came to hiring outside advice to get their way with the Coastal Commission, County largess knew no bounds. A San Diego lobbyist had been replaced by the Port of San Diego as the result of an injudicious e-mail in which she boasted that she could 'spoon feed' Coastal commissioners. The fact that she had blotted her copy book in San Diego didn't upset Los Angeles County or its Beaches and Harbors Department one bit. If she could spoon feed Coastal Commissioners as she said that was exactly the lady they wanted. They hired her too. At taxpayer expense, of course.

But the mere passing of the years worked in the County's favor too. People were replaced, promises were forgotten. This was not the case with the County which remained unflinching in its efforts to gain unimpeded control over Marina assets.

The biggest change was the retirement of Peter Douglas. Terminally ill with cancer he retired from the post before the Oceanside amendment hearing and was therefore no longer beholden to explaining to the public why he had dropped the promises he had exacted from Los Angeles County in 1996. Six other commission posts had been replaced by new faces in 2011.

Also of considerable significance was the refusal of the California Senate to reappoint Sara Wan to the Commission post she had held since 1996. The County undoubtedly saw Sara Wan as a hurdle for getting all it wanted from the Commission. Once again luck was with the County. She told me that her unpopularity in Malibu together with a campaign mounted against her in Sacramento probably resulted in her being dropped. A former state senator sent Wan a strongly worded letter accusing her of double-crossing Commissioner Mary Shallenberger in securing her reelection as Commission chairperson. Wan denied the accusation, saying she had not actively campaigned for re-nomination. But her victory in being reelected to the chair was short-lived. The Senate appointed someone else in her place when her term expired and with Wan gone, Shallenberger got the post.

The outcome of the 2011 hearing was left almost completely in the hands of the commission staff.

CHAPTER EIGHTEEN

The WOZ Overlay

The long reign of Peter Douglas over the California Coastal Commission drew to a close as the time for consideration of the Marina del Rey Local Coastal Program approached. Charles Lester, a senior executive of the Commission, was appointed Acting Executive Director in August 2011 when Douglas announced his retirement, and full-time Executive Director in September, barely two months before the meeting on the Marina. Douglas died of lung cancer the following April.

Lester's service with the Coastal Commission stretched back to 1997. He had previously been an Assistant Professor of Political Science at the University of Colorado. He left the formulation of the 2011 staff presentation on the amendment to the Deputy Director in charge of the southern region, Jack Ainsworth. Mr. Ainsworth was helped in his work by Commission Coastal Analyst Al Padilla. Padilla's contributions should have been most useful as he was actively involved in formulation of the 1996 amendment.

It is worth recalling what exactly was agreed between Los Angeles County and the California Coastal Commission in 1996 and what was incorporated as an amendment to the Marina Coastal Program binding on both sides. In 1996 the County promised to turn a parcel on the Marina west side into a park and to retain another parcel on the Washington Avenue fringe of the Marina as a parking lot. They agreed to keep 12.7 acres on the western side of the Marina as open space, even though more than eight acres of this was the water-logged part of the Oxford Flood Retention Basin and was of no possible public recreational use.

Coastal Commission staff, in making its recommendations for a further amendment in 2011, proceeded as if 1996 had never happened. It simply wiped the slate clean of all the binding agreements made in the previous amendment and started afresh.

Gone was the park on Lot FF promised in return for the County being granted 1,000 additional residential units in the area.

Gone was the parking lot on Washington Boulevard dubbed OT which the County had promised to retain as parking in return for keeping control of the last major unbuilt lot in the Marina and now demanded anew to make it a residential unit.

Gone was most of the usable open space mandated in the 1996 accords.

Gone was the protection of the parking lots which the 1996 agreement stipulated SHALL only be used for parks or parking.

Still very firmly in place, of course, were all the concessions, the concessions the County had been granted in 1996 including the 1,000 extra residential units and control over the last remaining major building lot.

Ainsworth began his presentation to commissioners by stating there were originally six projects in the Pipeline but two had been withdrawn. They were the conversion of the Mother's Beach picnic tables and parking lot into two hotels and the takeover of the boater's Mother's Beach parking lot. As these had been in public use for decades, this was scarcely an act of very great generosity on the part of the County or Coastal Commission.

Before proceeding to a discussion on the four remaining Pipeline projects Ainsworth said that another matter had come before the commission — that was its decision to hold the Marina hearing in Oceanside — a good four hours drive from the Marina itself and at a weekday hearing when few Los Angeles residents could afford to take the time off to make the trip through the choked coastal traffic. The staff opted for Oceanside even though a Commission meeting was scheduled for Los Angeles two months later when area residents could more easily attend. Although he did not mention it, three of the requests to postpone the hearing to a later date in Los Angeles County itself were from the State Senator for the region, the State Assembly Representative and the Los Angeles City Councilman whose district abutted the Marina and whose residents believed they would be affected by the proposed Marina developments. The difficulty which making the trip to Oceanside presented to many opponents of the amendment was rather pathetically illustrated by Kathy Knight of the Ballona Institute Education Program. "Please postpone any decision," she pleaded. "A lot of people wanted to come today and they couldn't. It was hard for me to get off time. We had to rent a car because our cars couldn't make it. There's a big recession. It costs a lot of money to get down here — gas, expenses, everything. So please don't make a decision until this can be finished in Los Angeles County."

But Mr. Ainsworth's heart was not to be melted by the pleas of ladies struggling with sputtering clunkers. "We did not think it was unreasonable to schedule these items for a hearing in Oceanside, which is considered a Southern California location," he told commissioners.

After eliminating the two Mother's Beach proposals from the Pipeline pro-

posals, Mr. Ainsworth went on to discuss the other four. Practically every assertion he makes in supporting these four County proposals is open to challenge.

To begin with the promised park (FF) so dear to Carla's heart, Mr.
Ainsworth said: "Now there has been considerable controversy regarding the
conversion of Parcel FF from Open Space designation to Residential designation....In Staff's opinion this parcel... would not make an attractive public
park for visitors to Marina del Rey."

"Now, some of the residents in the area argue that this parcel would make
a nice community park. Although it would provide a convenient community
park for the residents, that is not the user group the Commission is mandated
to serve pursuant to the recreation and access policies of the Coastal Act."

On his assertion that Parcel FF would not make a suitable public park,
Mr. Ainsworth was completely wrong. This parcel is a relatively flat space
which could be easily graded and converted to basketball and handball courts
and other youth-serving facilities which are almost completely lacking in the
Marina. It could also provide some parking for a huge area of the Marina
stretching along three moles, which, when the apartment block is built, will
have almost no space for public parking.

On the second point of it being a park for residents, Mr. Ainsworth need
only check the 1996 records to see that is precisely why the Commission demanded the provision of this park. Commission staff ruled that it was necessary to provide mitigation for 1,000 more residential units being permitted in
the area and the County went along with this proposal. Also it was pointed
out at the hearing that County code regulations required four acres of park for
every 1,000 residential units.

Mr. Ainsworth was obliged to return to the issue of the promised park later in the hearing when Commissioner Esther Sanchez, an Oceanside councilwoman, prompted by Carla's impassioned plea to save the promised park, said:
"There was a speaker — I'm sorry I didn't catch the name — that talked about
and used the terminology of an underutilized park and indicated that the park
was supposed to have been used as mitigation...Was that, in fact, initially considered mitigation ...and was the park directed to be developed there?"

Mr. Ainsworth responded that was the intention at that time.

"So the community thought that they had a promise of a park there
specifically?' Sanchez said.

Mr. Ainsworth's response: "That was their perception."

Perception!!!! Mr. Ainsworth. What about Map 5 in the 1996 LCP which
shows the lot as a park and County's concurrence with building the park.

On the question of the Coastal Improvement Fund which was supposed to
provide the moneys for building the park, Mr. Ainsworth told Commissioner

Sanchez: "Well, only — what is it, $35,000 has been collected to date because there's been no development in Marina del Rey, and there hasn't been enough money to really develop a park."

This misinforming of the Commissioners — there was actually $193,000 in the fund as Mr. Ainsworth spoke — must be regarded as an extremely serious matter as it undoubtedly put off Commissioner Sanchez from pursuing the subject and may have sunk the last chance of getting the promised park.

Mr. Ainsworth went on: "Now we're reevaluating that and looking at moving the park as part of Chace Park. (Miles away across the water from the promised park site.) The other mitigation would be at the wetland park."

Mr. Ainsworth's assertion that a nearby small wetland could in any way substitute for the promised park borders on the ridiculous. The 'wetland park' (Mr. Ainsworth had dropped into the habit of using County Waldos or 'queerings' — wetland park for wetland and underutilized parking lot for undeveloped park) was the remaining vestiges of an abandoned hotel project. Blocks of cement foundations poked up from its crater-like hole. The lot had been fenced in for decades. Rain collected in it during rainy season and water birds were attracted to it. The County wanted to remove this eyesore abutting two hotels it planned to construct on the lot by filling the hole with tidal water. The flooding project was clearly of great benefit to the developers of the two hotels but what benefit the public would get from it, if any, was not clear. However Mr. Ainsworth did see public benefits. "The wetland park would not only provide enhanced protection of this wetland area but it would also provide educational and *interpretive opportunities for the public who would be strolling by on the public promenade.*" (The italics are mine.)

As a final blow to the public park, Mr. Ainsworth announced that the moneys in the Coastal Improvement Fund, together with future builders' contributions, were to be diverted to flooding the wetland hole. (And, of course, providing educational and interpretive opportunities for the strolling public.)

Turning to the parking lot on Washington Boulevard which the County promised to keep as open space in 1996 but now proposed to turn into senior citizen apartments, Mr. Ainsworth said this space was unsuitable for a park because it was right next to the Oxford Flood Retention Basin which often stank and was clipped between two very busy roadways.

He then ruled out a list of other possible uses for the lot including hotels which were in overabundant supply in the area, a restaurant because the site was not waterfront, and boat storage because moving trailered boats in and out would interfere with the already heavy traffic in that area.

The one use Mr. Ainsworth did not mention was the one that was proposed years before and mentioned several times since then. That was to put a youth hostel on the lot. In 1995 Commission staffer Pam Emerson said: "The County recommends it for residential. …Staff is recommending that it be retained for parking, with a possible conditional use as a youth hostel."

Throughout the Marina history little or no attention had been paid to attracting youth to non-boating activities of the Marina, and none at all to providing reasonably-priced hotel accommodations for backpacking teenagers. As a result the Marina had taken on a somewhat sclerotic tone. Rents and condo fees were high and tended to attract well-to-do seniors. Even the affordable housing units which developers included in their buildings to facilitate getting building permits usually went to seniors. Mother's Beach, which had picnic tables for families and playgrounds for the kiddies, had only three or four volley ball nets to offer as youth recreation. And throughout the entire Marina those few volley ball nets were the only land-side amenities offered to youth.

Mr. Ainsworth concluded by saying that the senior housing was the best possible use for the OT lot. "We think the senior housing use is a good, smart growth use for this site by providing another option for housing in the Marina for seniors. And this use will generate much less traffic and parking demands."

But will it? Probably to relieve the developer of any need to provide facilities for the elderly (like the vanishing gourmet meals at the Monte Carlo senior apartments, for instance) the County created an entirely new land use designation for this lot — Active Seniors. Now one thing about Active Seniors is that they all have their cars — His and Hers. But when it came to required parking needs on the lot the County switched its vision of these seniors to tottering oldies who could no longer tell the difference between a brake and an accelerator. Calculating that these seniors would have reduced parking needs, it permitted a very reduced amount of parking for the 114 units, situating 94 required parking spaces on another lot three fifths of a mile away. If Mr. Ainsworth was looking for Marina visitors who did not require parking, he should have reverted to the original suggestion that the lot be used for a youth hostel. Backpackers don't have cars. They use public transport or they just walk to their hostels.

But perhaps the most important change contained in the 2011 amendment was that it removed the protection given to parking lots, essential for providing public access to the publicly-owned Marina. David Barish, co-director of WeAREMarina del Rey, addressed this crucial question in his presentation to the Commissioners. "The County is removing the major broad protection policy of parking lots that says parking lots can only be used for parking and a park," he said. "Why are we removing that whole broad policy if we're only converting a couple of parcels today?"

Barish complained of the County removing other critical protections. "They're removing a text on traffic cap, which says that development is based on traffic capacity. That's being deleted, so that's pretty major." He claimed that the County was using outdated and understated trip rates to artificially inflate development potential in the Marina.

"The Marina is public land for public recreation," he said. "It was created for that purpose, not for residential, not for commercial, and was paid for by taxpayer money from the County, the State and the U.S. government."

Finally Mr. Ainsworth turned to a large area on the eastern or inland side of the Marina which contained boat launch, boater parking and boat storage. And here we get to learn about that technicality with the strange name of the WOZ OVERLAY.

What exactly does this weird anagram represent? You may guess that because of all the concessions made to the County up to this point, it has something to do with giving more away to the County and in that you would be right. A WOZ (or Waterfront Overlay Zone) hands control over land use in the designated area to the County and takes oversight away from the Coastal Commission. And the County has already announced its intention of replacing boating facilities in this area with shopping malls.

After less than an hour of staff presentations, a great deal of which was devoted to bird life, the hearing moved on to public comment and to comments from the commissioners themselves. Within a matter of hours the fate of the publicly-owned Marina was sealed. The Commissioners' comments showed they had almost no prior knowledge of the history of the Marina LCP. They voted eleven to one for the proposed amendment, Commissioner Sanchez being the sole stand out. And with that simple vote, further large areas of the Marina had been privatized in virtual perpetuity and the County had acquired unimpeded authority on building caps and to determine land uses over remaining parking lots and the Wonderful World of WOZ.

Longtime commissioner Steve Blank had earlier predicted that when Peter Douglas retired the Coastal Commission would simply implode. "Once he's gone this Commission will implode in a blink of an eye."

The Commission vote was a shattering setback for all those who had fought for years to ensure public recreation and access within the Marina. As I emerged from the Commission hearing I got a vivid picture of just how bad the situation was. Nancy Marino was sitting on a bench in the foyer, her head sunk, looking absolutely destroyed. Over the years she had attended most of the meetings the County held on permitting the various Pipeline projects, she had gone to council meetings in neighboring districts to inform residents there on what the County proposed. And all her work had gone for nothing in a few hours. Her co-director on WeAREMarina del Rey, David Barish, was also deeply disheartened by the Commission vote. He came to a decision to resign from his Marina activities. "I can't imagine that anything is going to stop the County from doing exactly what it wants to do," he told me.

That vision of Nancy's face stays with me still. But the reason for her destroyed look can be easily explained.

She had just witnessed an implosion.

CHAPTER NINETEEN

A No-Show

Kathy Knight and her friends in the Ballona Institute Education Program had trouble finding a car that was capable of making the nearly 100 mile trip from Los Angeles to Oceanside for the November 3, 2011 Coastal Commission meeting.

It is hard to believe that the *L.A.Times* with its large fleet of motor vehicles was unable to find a car capable of making the journey.

Yet there was no *L.A.Times* reporter at the Oceanside meeting.

And, to the best of my knowledge, to this day the *L.A.Times* has never told its readers that at that meeting large areas of valuable publicly owned ocean-side land smack in the middle of Los Angeles' west side were handed over to private developers.

CHAPTER TWENTY

The Crown Jewel

Los Angeles County officials are so carried away by their rhetoric in describing the Marina as the 'crown jewel' of the county and lauding the number of times they have reached out to the public that they are probably incapable of seeing the brutal truth that lies behind the 2011 amendment. And that is that it is a trail of broken promises and of substituting residential and commercial development, low options under the California Coastal Act, for public recreation and parks, parking and open space.

The one who really goes overboard about the crown jewel is Supervisor Don Knabe, whose district includes the Marina. "Most of you have heard me call the Marina the crown jewel of Los Angeles County," he told the commissioners at Oceanside. "For our residents, boaters, visitors, it's an incredible, extraordinary destination for recreation and leisure.

"We come before you today with a vision. Not of piecemeal development, but a vision for the Marina that will turn it into a destination location not just for existing residents and boaters but for all visitors and residents of Los Angeles County and across the country.

"We have done an incredible outreach program with our staff. Since 2008 we have held 79 public meetings, we have had public reviews at our board meetings, and we have established community working groups. And that is on top of the hundreds and hundreds of meetings that we've had with individuals, stakeholders, community, and boating groups.

"AND WE LISTENED!!"

Yet the County's record of listening is a particularly bad one. Set aside the two Mother's Beach private developments which all agree never should have been in the Phase II in the first place, add to that the expansion of Burton Chace Park, a bonus the County received from the original Wisniewski Phase II which planned to dump Mother's Beach picnickers and boaters there, the 2011 amendment is a total victory of private development over public recreation and for County assertion of its exclusive authority over parks, building caps and WOZ-covered land use.

The County refused to listen when the *Los Angeles Times*, in a well-informed series of articles, said the 39-year lease extensions of favored lessees at firesale prices were a giveaway of precious publicly-owned land and urged that the proposed extended leases by reviewed.

The most flagrant example of the County's refusal to listen was its rejection of the advice of qualified architects and urban planners they themselves had appointed to the Marina Design Control Board. These experts met within the Marina itself and held night-time meetings to allow for the maximum input of County citizens. The Supervisors, objecting to some of the recommendations of the board including their condemnation of the boat stacking tower, eviscerated its powers. Richard Bruckner, Director of County Regional Planning, working from a downtown office, became the gatekeeper for advancing development projects. Bruckner was one of the County speakers at the Oceanside meeting and he was lavish, too, with his encomiums about what the County was planning in the Marina. "We are very excited about the opportunity to.... polish that jewel, take another look at the Marina, meet with the public, and revision the area."

But the County had not heard the last words of advice from the Design Control Board.

Peter Phinney, appointed chair of the board after Susan Cloke's resignation, is a nominee of Supervisor Don Knabe, and therefore might be assumed to be reluctant about criticizing his nominator. But Phinney's statement at a February 17, 2010, meeting of the board was strongly critical of what the County was doing.

He said over his five years of service on the board he had talked with a lot of people and he had found they did not trust the County. "Public trust does not exist here," he said. "There's a real profound lack of public trust.

"I think initially the Marina was created as a public benefit to provide recreation for the people of Los Angeles County and its clearly owned by the 8 or 10 million people, the residents of the County, not the 10 thousand people who live here but the County as a whole, and it existed to provide access to the water.

"The County supervisors then were really the trustees of that asset," Phinney said. But the County, instead of checking development decisions against the need to provide citizen's access to the water and recreation, had allowed itself to be driven by the development community and the desire for immediate budget fixes, he said.

"I'm not sure how we found ourselves in this kind of predicament but the fact is now that development in the Marina has been driven by the development community's willingness to risk its money for future profit...It's the development community that's paying for all these re-developments at the Marina."

To applause from the people attending the board meeting, Phinney con-cluded. "There isn't a check against what that's doing to the public resource for voters and access to the water. So it's a real concern and I think that that's some-thing the County needs to remain focused on in its response at this point. And I think we also need to think as a group, not as a commission but as a group of concerned members of the County about ways that we can begin to recapture the focus on the recreational aspects."

Unlike Mrs. Cloke, Phinney was not subsequently placed in a position of feeling forced to resign. The Supervisors probably thought that as his board was no longer in a position to throw a spanner in the works they could safely allow him to let off steam.

Another prime example of the County's penchant for not listening was its habit of hiring urban planning companies to provide studies on Marina recre-ation whenever it regarded this as politically expedient. RRM Design Group did a study on Burton Chace Park in 2008. That same group did a study on Mother's Beach in 2006 and Gruen Associates did another Mother's Beach study in 2010. They came up with glamorous drawings of proposed recreation-al ideas which were projected on screens at public meetings. Yet the moment their projectors were turned off, that was it. None of their ideas were ever put into effect.

With exclusive say over most land uses in the Marina safely under its belt, the County turned to trying to demonstrate it had the interests of rec-reation seekers at heart all along. Two paddle board rentals and a row boat franchise popped up on Mother's Beach. Improvised pack drill gyms sprang up round the edge of the beach with the bark of the pack drill instructors merg-ing with the bark of the seals across the waters. Beaches and Harbor's offi-cials revived a project for building a pedestrian track around the Oxford Flood Retention Basin. But this was not new. It was one of the two recreational proj-ects promised in 1996 along with the public park on parcel FF. The fact that the County came up with millions of dollars to pay for it in 2013 shows that their assertion they had never had money to pay for the park on FF is a particularly bad joke. The reason why the flood retention track got the go-ahead is abun-dantly clear. You can't build revenue-producing apartment blocks on a mud flat which is periodically inundated by rainstorms.

As the Oceanside meeting County officials made much of the Visioning Process by which County residents would be invited to participate in plan-ning the future of the Marina. But as every available lot had been given away for long-term private development it was not clear what exactly was left to Vision. Jon Nahhas, the boating advocate who by this stage was one of the last defenders of the recreational Marina left standing, contacted the County official in charge of visioning and was told a visioning tour in which citizens were invited to participate would not include the west or ocean side of the Marina. He objected strenuously, saying that most of the controversial projects were on this side of the Marina. But the County adhered to the very limited tour and participants were shown only a few possibilities for development on the inland side.

As a final word on the County's "visioning" process. I quote an ordinary citizen who nevertheless kept a close watch on what was happening from her tower condominium on the city side of the Marina. I met Roz Walker when she made a contribution to our WeAREMarinadelRey activities but lost touch with her thereafter. Recently I saw her quoted in an *Argonaut* article on the County's "visioning" process. Her words: "They have approved so many projects here and not listened to us for years, so the idea of visioning makes me laugh and sick to my stomach at the same time. No one in the county listens to us, so in my opinion this is just a bunch of baloney."

While making much of its visioning exercise, the County was time and time again siding with developers to advance its schemes for the over-development of the residential and commercial Marina. David Barish had kept a close watch on the patch of wetland near his apartment for some time because he suspected that the wetland area, as measured by certain native plants, was actually expanding. But what eventually came to his attention was a total surprise. The County, bent on permitting the construction of two five-story hotels on the same large lot, had actually allowed one of the hotels to intrude on the wetland. As Barish told the Oceanside Coastal Commission meeting: "Per the Coastal Act Section 30233, you cannot move a wetland for development purposes… You can't do that."

However the County went right ahead with its wetland moving plans. It went to another Coastal Commission meeting to get approval from what had become a very accommodating Commission. But by this time citizens had had enough of the County doing exactly what it wanted. They sued in Los Angeles court to stop the wetland juggling and their case is still waiting to be heard.

As already noted, the Doug Ring organization had twice been let off the hook for failing to start work on a project known as Esprit 2 by the contractual date. But the second time round, the County supervisors made a major concession to Ring. It authorized the company to flip its ownership on Esprit 1, a prime waterside complex with a magnificent view of the entire Marina main channel. County officials stated that this was "the largest real estate deal of the year in Southern California." On an initial investment of $102 million at its opening in 2008 the company had realized a final sale of $225 million just five years later. Jon Nahhas again leapt into the fray. "Esprit LLC was allowed to profit nearly $100 million at the taxpayers' expense on the public lands of Marina del Rey," he said. He claimed the County had approved the resale without going through the proper process allowing for public comment and opposition, and he said if the supervisors failed to remedy the situation he would sue and ask the judge to order County to pay court costs and reasonable attorney fees.

Then, out of the blue, the County announced it planned to shift the recreational boaters' launch ramp from its calm spot at the headwaters of the Marina to a much trickier launch site on the heavily trafficked main channel. The decision was promptly denounced by a commissioner on the County's boating review board whose members are appointed by the County's Board of Supervisors themselves. Commissioner Dave Lumian of the Small Craft Harbor Commission warned that the move would create problems for boaters. "From a boating perspective , it's almost laughable," he said.

The decision to shift the public launch ramp underscored the disregard the County had shown for Marina recreation throughout.

It had tried to push the picnickers off Mother's Beach to a site on the other side of the Marina where there was no sand for their children to play. The protest of the picnickers put a stop to that one.

They had tried to close down the sandy launch spot for non-powered boaters on Mother's Beach by giving away access from their parking lot across the road. The rowers and kayakers had turned out to protest that the deepwater launch site the County proposed was unsafe and again the County was forced to yield.

The Coastal Commission had ruled in 1996 that open space be retained for recreation on the FF lot and that a parking lot be preserved on the OT to provide for access. The County grabbed both lots for apartment developments in 2011 and ruled that the public had to be content with two areas which were almost completely water-logged and of no recreational use whatever (that is if 'recreation' is accorded its usual meaning of basketball, handball, tennis, swimming, athletics etc.)

Their decision to move the launch ramp, so beloved by weekend sailors, capped a long history of the County's mishandling of the recreational Marina.

The reason for the move was fairly obvious. The County wanted to clear the area of boating facilities around the launch ramp so it could install a much more profitable shopping mall. In effect the launch ramp was being re-located, probably at taxpayer expense, to accommodate a few irrelevant boutique shops.

As this book was about to go to print, the County dropped another bombshell.

It planned to permit the refurbishing and lease extension on a village-style apartment complex on the picturesque northern side of the Marina inlet known as Mariner's Village.

There was only one problem with this rebuilding scheme. This complex of 28 low-level residential units inset with gardens and bunches of tall trees is the last refuge of the Great Blue Heron in the Marina. By cutting down all the existing trees and undertaking a noisy rebuilding over ten years — herons don't like noise — the project threatened to drive out the herons completely.

As bird painter Jean-Jacques Audubon showed so effectively, the Great Blue Heron is one of the most beautiful of God's creations. At nesting time when the herons glide along the waterfront of Mariner's Village one behind the other, they turn the skyline of the Marina into a Japanese scroll painting.

The Great Blue Herons are clearly an asset for Marina del Rey in making it a wild life refuge and a tourist attraction. Yet the birds have met with nothing but hostile actions on the part of the County and its lessees.

The birds' troubles in the Marina began in 2000 with what became popularly known as the 'heron wars'. The owners of the apartment block Villa Venetia across the waters on the southern side of the Marina inlet objected to the clucking sound the herons made during nesting and the layer of white guano manure it deposited on their roadways. But their main objection was that the herons stood in the way of their construction plans.

They tried to sneak in a tree cutting team early one morning. But from an upper level apartment in their building a heron lover was watching. When the tree cutters' bulldozers arrived on the scene they were blocked by scores of opponents. One hardy protester even climbed a tree to force them to back off. Newspaper reporters and photographers turned up. State and County authorities were called in and an agreement was reached that there would be no cutting or trimming of trees in heron nesting season.

With a change of ownership and the fact that the heron wars story gradually lost its media pizzazz, the Villa Venetia was eventually able to get what it wanted. In two tree cutting events popularly known as "Chainsaw Massacre I" and "Chainsaw Massacre II" they succeeded in cutting down the rookery trees.

The nesting herons were driven out of the Villa Venetia area and took up residence in Mariner's Village across the way, joining other herons who had been nesting at this site since the late 1980's.

The brutal assault on the heron rookeries stirred an unfavorable public reaction. The California Coastal Commission took up the defense of the rookeries. A Commission official stated: "We are fully prepared to intervene if anyone pulls out their chainsaws." In 2008 the Marina herons were given the very highest of wildlife protection under the California Coastal Act. Their nesting and roosting sites were designated as Endangered Species Habitat Areas (ESHA).

But in October 2011 after a new director took over at the Coastal Commission, an intense lobbying effort by the County and its lessees resulted in the ESHA protection being withdrawn.

In its place both County and lessees promised they would continue to support protections given to the herons.

Yet, as with most County undertakings, these promises were almost immediately broken. The heron wars were about to begin anew. Mariner's Village soon after engaged in a stealth war of trimming trees and cutting out heron's nests. One Mariner's Village renter heard tree cutting being done at midnight. The plans that the owners of Mariner's Village put to the the Marina Design Control Board in March 2014 called for the removal of every existing tree in the village.

To its everlasting credit, the Design Control Board unanimously rejected the Mariner's Village plan and called for the lessees to come back with another plan which took into account public objections. But with the Design Control Board no longer in a position to impose its will, having been stripped of its initial review powers by the County in 2008, Marina residents expect that the County will rapidly lose patience with the Design Control Board and push through the Mariner's Village proposals at a higher level.

Despite the setbacks the heron population has suffered — experts say nests in 2014 will probably be down by half from their peak — Marcia Hanscom, a leading heron supporter, remains eternally optimistic the County will recognize the importance of the herons as a wildlife tourist attraction and will move to protect their rookeries.

The scores of people I talked to while researching this book faulted the County on two major points. The first was that it had failed to maintain a proper balance between recreation and private development in its plans for the Marina. The second was that it had done a lousy job of negotiating with the lessees and many described its lease extensions as 'gifts'. They are certainly right on the first point and the figures bear them out on the second.

As I see it, looking through my Jake Gittes 'Chinatown' shades, the recreational Marina was given away to private interests for a mere trickle of revenue. The current thirty million dollars a year or thereabouts barely covers the Mad Money the supervisors are allocated each year for their pet projects. The lessees scoop up the shekels.

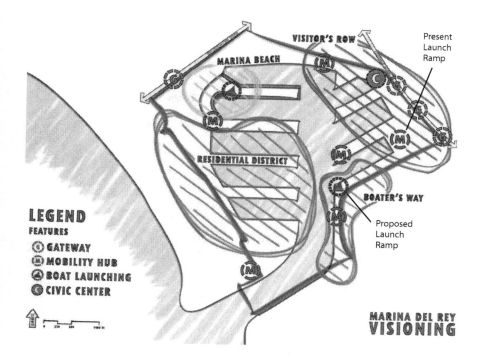

LEGEND
FEATURES
- ⓖ GATEWAY
- ⓜ MOBILITY HUB
- ⓐ BOAT LAUNCHING
- ⓒ CIVIC CENTER

Present Launch Ramp

Proposed Launch Ramp

**MARINA DEL REY
VISIONING**

THE COUNTY'S 'VISIONING' PROCESS
What the Circles Mean (without the County's spin)

The "Residential District" Circle

Huge area of coastal side of the Marina given over to apartment blocks, the lowest option for development under the California Coastal Act, with little or no mitigation as required by the Coastal Commission.

County creating a forbidding neighborhood of high walls and guarded or digi-coded entrances with no provision for motorcar parking or even waiting. The perceived impression will be 'Visitors Keep Out'.

The "Visitors Row" Circle

This area, at present occupied, by boatyards, boating facilities and the public launch ramp is to be converted to shops, totally unneeded in a neighborhood which is probably the most heavily shopped area in southern California — five supermarkets within walking distance of each other and the Costco store on top of that. Prepare for traffic snarls.

The "Boaters' Way" Circle

Boating facilities including the relocated public launch ramp crammed into half the area. Boater's Way to be dominated by a massive boat stacking tower looming over the natural panorama of the Ballona Wetlands and sticking out 100 ft over the water.

CHAPTER TWENTY-ONE

My Vision

Lest this work be considered an exercise in negativism, let me offer some Visioning of my own.

Looking eastward from the ocean, the area of Venice Peninsula and Marina del Rey forms a large block of land divided into strips like a Mille Feuilles pastry. The Venice Peninsula part of it belongs to the City and the publicly-owned Marina is managed by the County. (It may be helpful at this point to refer to the map in the front of the book.)

Working in from the ocean the first strip is, of course, the Venice Peninsula beach. This is a wide swathe of sand stretching just under a mile southward from the crowded alleys of Venice to the wide inlet which furnishes the waters of Ballona Creek, the Marina and Abbot Kinney's original main canal which fed his Venice grid of waters. The beach is not exploited as fully as it might be by recreation seekers because the property owners who have their houses and apartment blocks along the sand's edge have shown a tendency towards Malibu-itis — that is defending their right to control public uses of the peninsula down to the last legal brief. They have opposed extending a bicycle trail down the beach to the Marina inlet and they have fought against the completion of a promenade in front of their houses. I am not entirely without sympathy for their objections as I will explain later. Part of the extreme southern portion of the beach is fenced off as a breeding space for a bird species called the Lesser Tern and within the fences the beach has reverted to its original form of dunes spiked by tufts of grass. A drawback to being so close to the Ballona Creek entrance is that in the rainy season the trash of Los Angeles City gets swept out into the ocean and then back on to the beach requiring a major clean up lasting over a period of days. Oil seepage from the ocean floor and possibly from boats illegally discharging their old oil can form black globs on the sand at times, making bare-foot jogging a hazard. The peninsula is mainly the preserve of joggers and long-distance walkers. A very limited population lives along the beach edge so it is rare to see the sand much used.

The next layer is a strip of houses and apartment blocks stretching as little as a hundred yards inland in most parts and bordered to the east by Pacific Avenue. The series of narrow alleys which run from the avenue through to the beach have been given attractive marine names in alphabetical order — Anchorage, Buccaneer, Catamaran, Driftwood etc. — but not quite making it to Z for Zephyr which is called the Main Canal Inlet. During the days of the California oil boom this strip was dotted with donkey engine drills with their bobbing heads pumping up the oil from beneath the sands. The last of these drills disappeared in the late nineteen hundreds and real estate development took over. Fears are occasionally raised that the oil wells were not adequately capped and that there could be a seepage of explosive methane gas from beneath the houses. As I have said, the residents of Venice Peninsula beach have resolutely opposed any extension of the coastal bike path or pedestrian promenade down their beach. They understandably fear that either of these pathways could bring the drug dealers and purveyors of stolen goods from the Venice boardwalk down into their tranquil neighborhood. The result is that there is no bike trail down the beach and the promenade is a ridiculous stop-and-start of a wide cement walkway illuminated with handsome street lamps cut off by areas where there is no path, no lighting and walkers have to slog their way through sand, often having to detour round the deck chairs and gardens of residents who have taken over the intended promenade area as their own space.

The next layer is Abbot Kinney's main canal which has been allowed to fall into an unsightly state of disrepair with rotting timbers and blocks of cement poking up from its waters. The main canal also forms a barrier for people further inland getting to the beach. In its near mile length there is only one bridge – that is at the letter L or Lighthouse Street. Why there are so few bridges and the reason for the sorry state of the canal is hard to decipher. The barrier of the Main Canal is one of the principal causes for the dyslectic development of the whole area and for the spats between County and City officials which can be acrimonious. Additional bridges at H for Hurricane and R for Reef are absolutely essential.

Over the other side of the Main Canal is another strip of City territory and the way this has been developed is a tremendous credit to the City. It is comprised of handsome single family homes, many of them of considerable architectural interest. Between rows of houses the City has planted little garden malls. And along the Canal a path has been reserved for pedestrians who can study the houses and gardens and observe the bird life in the water. Wow!! The only drawback is that pedestrians are unable to break away to get to the beach without tramping to either end of the mile-or-so long path. And even if they could get to the beach, no proper beachside promenade awaits them.

The next strip is the main drag of Via Marina which is the divide between

City and County for most, but not all, of its length. At the beginning and the end of Via Marina, County territory is on both sides of the Marina. This has caused a major problem to arise between the City and County over the building over a main drainage pipe between Venice and points south. The city wants the pipe to go along Via Marina. The County opposes this and has taken its objections all the way up to the Supreme Court. Via Marina is a car speedway with not many more traffic controls than the Main Canal has bridges. Pedestrians crossing it do so at the risk of their lives for much of its length. There is also no bicycle path. So added to the fact that the beach residents have nixed a bicycle path on the beach, the message is pretty clear that cyclists are not wanted in Venice Peninsula.

Inland from Via Marina lies the Marina proper.

This layering and division of jurisdictions has resulted in a development process in which recreational interests are disregarded on both sides. On the County side recreation is being squeezed by over development. On the city side, the laissez faire attitude of city officials bending unduly to the wishes of the beach dwellers has had an equally harmful effect. My feeling is that if this state of affairs continues it will result in the Marina/Venice Peninsula area being written off by Los Angeles' population as overcrowded, overtrafficked and inaccessible.

I believe that if the Marina/Venice Peninsula area is to be made into a true tourist attraction (and not just the polished gem of County officials imaginings which is supposed to lure tourists to its incandescent gleam) City and County officials have to bury their hatchets and get together to plan the development of their joint territory.

I have been largely critical of the County during this work but it must be admitted that most of the work that remains to be done lies with the City. The main canal has to be cleaned up and a few more bridges put across it to encourage the residents of the Marina to use Venice Peninsula Beach. Once this is done, hotels on the County side have to emphasize that the Beach is only a few attractive steps away. If Venice Peninsula residents' objections to the promenade being completed all the way to the Venice boardwalk need to be taken into account at this point, then the city should at least complete the promenade from Lighthouse southward to the Marina entrance so City and County residents and visitors have an attractive walk rather than the ridiculous intermittent slug of cement and sand which they at present have to endure.

City and County need to set up a joint development committee with powers to rule on the suitability of projects for luring tourists. Such a committee would be something on the lines of the original Marina Design Control Board with city councillors and supervisors retaining the power to veto any project of which they disapprove. It would also have the effect of mitigating the power of developers to lead the County by the nose and of beach property owners dictating beach development policies to the City.

One project that springs immediately to mind is that a restored main canal could once again become the bearer of Abbot Kinney's gondolas. Hired gondolas and paddle boats could ply the calm waters of the canal, free of the boat traffic of the Marina itself. Then there is a rational development of the beachside promenade.

Having said what the City should do, let me return to the County. The Supervisors have a chance to redeem themselves by turning the area along Fiji Way on the south side of the Marina into a totally youth serving area. At present the plans are to erect an unsightly wall along the edge of the Ballona Wetlands consisting of the boat-stacking tower, another stretch of their abysmal apartment units, and a semi-circular building shown in the architectural mock-up as having a few tables and umbrellas and which is being touted as some sort equivalent of the French Riviera promenades. It is doubtful if many people are going to be tempted to drive past the boat-stacking tower to get to these outdoor tables, and the project has every chance of being as big a fiasco as the faux Fisherman's Village which it replaces. But a youth hostel, basketball and handball courts would attract a huge crowd of young people. And to pay for it all, the County could permit a number of very profitable youth cafes and nightclubs.

Epilogue

If this tale of the machinations of Los Angeles County government upsets you, you may yourself choose to get involved.

For one thing, not all of the County's giveaway plans are completely set in stone.

The County has acquired the power to do what it wants with parking lots and inevitably a number of parking lots will be up for grabs. When the County announces its plans for further giveaways to private developers, message the County on your opposition, call your local State assemblyman and senator and write letters to newspapers.

The aim of this book is to arm you with the facts to make your protest more effective.

For additional copies of this book contact **lulu.com**, local bookstores or online bookselling services.

Proceeds from book are dedicated to preserving and increasing recreational facilities in Marina del Rey.

For further details on extending Marina recreation, visit my Blog site at **marinadelrey-sellout.blogspot.com** or e-mail me at **selloutmdr@gmail.com**.

Bruce Russell
Marina del Rey

47598171R00058

Made in the USA
San Bernardino, CA
13 August 2019